BECOMING

How to Launch Your Design-Driven Ventures

A DESIGN

from Apps to Zines

ENTREPRENEUR

STEVEN HELLER & LITA TALARICO

SVA NYC

ALLWORTH PRESS
NEW YORK

All inquiries should be addressed to
Allworth Press
307 West 36th Street, 11th Floor
New York, NY 10018

Allworth Press books may be purchased in bulk at special discounts for sales promotion, corporate gifts, fund-raising, or educational purposes. Special editions can also be created to specifications. For details, contact the Special Sales Department.
Allworth Press
307 West 36th Street, 11th Floor
New York, NY 10018
or info@skyhorsepublishing.com.

20 19 18 17 16   5 4 3 2 1

PUBLISHED BY
Allworth Press, an imprint of Skyhorse Publishing, Inc.
307 West 36th Street, 11th Floor
New York, NY 10018
Allworth Press® is a registered trademark of Skyhorse Publishing, Inc.®,
a Delaware corporation.
www.allworth.com

COVER AND INTERIOR DESIGN BY
Anderson Newton Design

Library of Congress Cataloging-in- Publication Data is available on file.

Print ISBN: 978-1- 62153-508- 9
Ebook ISBN: 978-1- 62153-514- 0

Printed in China

DEDICATION

Nicolas Heller – SH

Julian Friedman – LT

Contents

Preface

When we began using the term "design entrepreneur," the two words were rarely uttered together. Now the next big thing in graphic design—in fact, in all design disciplines—is entrepreneurship. The United States is a land of inventors, and entrepreneurs and designers have virtually all the skills needed to conceive, develop, research, and produce—in short, *make*—products for a marketplace. What was missing when we began were business, presentation, and promotion expertise.

This book builds, in part, on the curriculum of The School of Visual Arts MFA Design/Designer as Author + Entrepreneur program (which we founded and co-chair). With the help of our faculty, alumni, and staff, we have fine-tuned this material for nearly twenty years. It is part handbook and part casebook, addressing how designers can accelerate their concepts as marketable in the analog and digital worlds.

Entrepreneurship is risky yet empowering. Taking ownership of ideas and fabrications, either alone or in collaboration with others, is a goal worth pursuing and an opportunity worth taking. Even failure is an opportunity. Entrepreneurship is a learning process. The designer must learn to incorporate design talent with business skill to ensure the outcome of any sustainable venture.

—SH + LT

Acknowledgments

First and foremost, we thank David Rhodes, president of the School of Visual Arts, for his continued support of design entrepreneurship throughout the school, and for his generosity to the MFA Design (MFAD) program and its students, past and present.

We are grateful to Tad Crawford, publisher of Allworth Press, for his unflagging enthusiasm for graphic design and design in general. This book is a tribute to his dedication.

Without our co-workers at MFAD, Esther Ro Schofield, director of operations, and Ron Callahan, technology director, we would be at a huge loss. Thank you for your dedication to our program and students. For their design and typography, thanks to Gail Anderson and Joe Newton of Anderson Newton Design.

Warm wishes to the faculty members, both current and past, who have added their own imprimaturs to design entrepreneurship, either by engaging in it themselves or encouraging others.

And to all those who were interviewed, analyzed, and otherwise probed about their entrepreneurial highs and lows, we are sincerely thankful for your generosity.

—SH + LT

An Entrepreneur's Glossary

TERMS IN CURRENT USE

ACCELERATOR Company that fast-tracks start-ups to launch their ventures

ANGEL Investor who looks for early-stage ventures to provide capital in exchange for equity in the venture

ANCILLARY An extra that adds to the core product of the venture in hopes that it will attract a target audience

ASSET Something that has value or can generate income

BRANDING The narrative that identifies a product, venture, or service

BRAND PLATFORM Items that define a product's core attributes

BUSINESS MODEL *(aka Value Exchange)* Definition of the product and how it will make a profit

COLLATERAL Different types of marketing products that support a venture

COLLABORATION Working with others to accomplish a task

CORE CONCEPT The idea that drives all the parts of a product

DECK Series of Keynote slides or PDFs showing key elements of a pitch or proposal

DELIVERING VALUE Promise of what you will provide to an audience

ECOSYSTEM *(see Stakeholder)* All the participants in a venture, from the creators and founders to the various stakeholders, who will provide sustenance and sustainability

END USER The intended audience for a product

ENTREPRENEUR Person who starts a new business venture that requires initiative and risk

ELEVATOR PITCH Quick summary used to define a product

ETHNOGRAPHY Research that is conducted to provide in-depth understanding of the culture of a targeted audience

EXPERIENCE Response a user has to a venture

FOUNDER Originator of the idea and creator of the venture

IDENTITY Look and feel of the product *(also Logo)*

INCUBATOR Entity that attempts to nourish potential ventures

INNOVATION Term used to describe new ventures

INTELLECTUAL PROPERTY Legal rights for protecting ideas including trademark, copyright, trade dress

ITERATION *(experimenting to iterate the experience)* Developing a version of the product

LOGO Identity mark of a company

MARKET TESTING Evaluating responses to a product prior to releasing it

MINIMUM VIABLE PRODUCT *(MVP)* Core elements of product that launches early for feedback in order to iterate

MISSION STATEMENT Essence of a business's goals and philosophy

PITCH Defining a venture in a way that excites and generates interest

PRODUCT End result that is offered to meet the needs of the intended audience

PRODUCT NARRATIVE Story behind the venture

PROTOTYPE Early iteration of a product

REFINEMENT Iterating and fine-tuning of the product

RESEARCH Substantiating assumptions and claims

SEED FUNDING Seeking an investor and raising money to launch a product

SERIAL ENTREPRENEUR Someone who starts new businesses and hands them off to someone else

SOCIAL ENTREPRENEUR Someone who develops products for public/social benefit

STAKEHOLDER Anyone with an interest in or who is affected by the product

START-UP Company or partnership that seeks out scalable business models

SUSTAINABILITY Ability to continually support the business aspect of the product

TECHNOLOGIST Engineer who works in collaboration with the designer

UMBRELLA TOPIC Broad and general term that can describe multiple and related ideas

UNICORN Start-up company whose valuation has exceeded $1 billion

USER EXPERIENCE Experiential effect a product will have on its audience

VALIDATION Testing the product for its viability

VALUE EXCHANGE *(aka Business Model)* Worth of the product or service

VALUE PROPOSITION Promise to be delivered to the customer by the product

VENTURE Launching a product when the outcome is uncertain and involves risk

VENTURE CAPITAL *(VC)* Money provided by investors for early-stage start-up businesses

Maker, Making, Made

Design entrepreneurship began more than a century ago. Today it is the answer to the question: What's next? Back in 1998, when we cofounded the School of Visual Arts MFA Design/Designer as Author + Entrepreneur program, the logical next evolutionary step for graphic designers was to become "content producers," just like our design ancestors from the Arts & Crafts, Werkbund, Bauhaus, and Charles and Ray Eames and other design movements, schools, and studios from the late nineteenth and early to mid-twentieth centuries.

It was becoming clear that the brief period from the late 1980s through the 1990s, when graphic design was promoted in media as a cultural force, was losing steam. The computer, which had shined its bright screen on flamboyant and experimental design that gave rise to designers with household name recognition, would eventually marginalize graphic designers in the bargain. It was time for a preemptive, radical shift transforming endangered graphic designers from service providers to idea "conceptualizers" to makers of the ideas they conceived. The design entrepreneur, therefore, applied conventional skill and talent to conceiving and producing new products.

Initially we used the term "author" to describe our MFA program because "design authorship" had a loftier ring than "entrepreneur." "Author" implied the freedom to conceptualize anything that was not client-driven—as long as it wasn't art for art's sake. "Entrepreneur," conversely, was as much about business as creativity. Despite an increase in professionalism during the 1970s and 1980s, the "b-word" (business) threatened some design artistes. For design authors, business strategies and plans were rejected or embraced, but were not a prerequisite. Being a design entrepreneur, however, demanded considerably more rigor in terms of business, marketing, and promotion savvy; it was important to maintain a balance of art and commerce.

> Any designer who runs a studio, office, or firm, is entrepreneurial.
> In fact, anyone with a studio already has the infastructure for entrepreneurial content development.

Any designer who runs a studio, office, or firm is entrepreneurial. In fact, anyone with a studio already has an infrastructure for entrepreneurial content development. But design entrepreneurship really picked up steam in the early 2000s when technology provided the tools for making stuff and opportunities for various "making" outcomes. While a lot of what's made —items like greeting cards or T-shirts—doesn't necessarily require high technology, the computer makes "making" matter-of-fact. It also enables makers to prototype, promote, and sell directly to consumers.

The surge in online markets, the capacity to reach customers and raise funds from modest investors through fund-sourcing sites, has forever altered how business is conducted. Right now, Internet entrepreneurs are developing more systems and structures that enable design entrepreneurs to dip into and benefit from new markets.

The ability to produce and market has helped to reposition graphic design in the new entrepreneurial economy. Which is not to imply that graphic design services are no longer necessary. To the contrary, these services are more necessary than ever, in part because design entrepreneurs are raising design bars and standards.

Entrepreneurship is not for everyone, yet everyone harbors at least one viable product idea. What's more, designers do not have to be profit-making; instead, they can be "social entrepreneurs," creating campaigns or events that serve the greater good. By virtue of their creative skill set, graphic designers are easily thrust into being entrepreneurial (individually or collaboratively).

Making is the new sketching. The prevailing ethos is to make first, test later. Once something is made, if it doesn't fly, simply make something else. The costs for putting prototypes into the world are minimal compared to the pre-computer/pre-Internet days. What's more, many entrepreneurial products today are digital, so start-up investment is manageable.

This may account for why so many designers are currently producing and distributing their own bespoke (custom or limited edition) products. The following is a selection of six ventures, from print publications to vinyl toys to a social-impact iPhone app that have found or are searching for their rightful audiences.

Design entrepreneurial ventures do not necessarily follow typical modus operandi. As many of the entrepreneurs described here note, their ideas derive from personal interests that are then universalized. Or there is an attempt to find an audience of like-minded people. Many products are finding space in the virtual world, but the ideas are concrete, if sometimes ethereal, at first glance. The overarching concern is not whether the product will make money—that will either come or not—but whether it will bring pleasure or do good or change attitudes. If not, then why bother? Everyone wants a hit, but a very smart miss will do just fine.

Design Entrepreneur First Venture Survival Tips

BY KEN CARBONE, PRINCIPAL, CARBONE SMOLAN AGENCY, NY

1. Keep the BIG picture in focus. Don't get lost in the details too soon. Keep the process fluid and moving forward. When you are stuck, change focus and concentrate on another issue. There is plenty to do.

2. Be careful of the generosity of others. To create a successful project often requires collaborators and consultants. Lock them in early. Make it easy for them to help. Have a fallback position should a collaborator drop out.

3. Define your customer as clearly and precisely as possible. A customer base defined as "everyone from 18 to 65" will get you nowhere. Start with the audience who will most benefit from your product or service. It's helpful to draw upon your own personal experience, peer group, and knowledge of a target market, then conduct additional research as necessary.

4. Be realistic in your balance of "skill & will." You might have a fabulous idea for space travel, but unless you are an astrophysicist, you will encounter daunting obstacles that will impede progress. Be realistic about your ability to successfully execute your concept.

5. Keep a close eye on the competitive landscape. There are a lot of great ideas out there and more arrive every day. A quick online search will reveal competitors in your space. However, this needn't be a deterrent. There is always the possibility that you can improve on an idea or business model, resulting in a product or service that offers increased value for a potentially different audience.

6. Less talk and more making builds momentum. Every venture requires thorough research, writing, and continuous refinement of its story. It's better to demonstrate your ideas through visual examples to stimulate meaningful and constructive dialogue.

7. He said, she said. At times you might hear conflicting advice from different people. Don't worry—it's all good. Just apply the best counsel that supports your objectives and keep moving forward.

8. What to do in a creative crisis? It happens to absolutely everyone. You hit a wall. The ideas stop coming. You panic. The next-best step is to stop everything, backtrack to where you started, think about what excited you in the beginning. There's a good chance things have gotten too complex. Try simplifying your offering. Narrow your audience. Reset your goals with added clarity. Not every idea has to change the world.

9. Let go. You thought the idea was brilliant. Early signs reinforced this, but for many creative, practical, budgetary, logistical, or scheduling reasons, the future looks bleak. Starting over is often the best plan of action.

10. S.O.S. If your venture is truly in distress, call for help EARLY.

An Entrepreneurial Toolkit

*The demands on today's entrepreneur require fluency
in a wide range of problems and solutions. Here are the skills that will
aid the in making and selling.*

CHAPTER ONE

From Idea to Product, Campaign, or Service

Before you can become an entrepreneur, you must make your concept into a bona fide entity.

Contemporary graphic, product, and interactive designers are working in the most advantageous time for being a part-time, full-time, or one-time design entrepreneur. This is your moment! You have tools for fundraising, making, and distributing, not to mention promoting and selling. The digital world has made production easier than ever before, yet the field has never been more crowded. So this chapter is aimed at bringing you to a level that extends your respective reaches.

Here's something to remember—a mantra, if you like: Think big, yet narrow your sights. Ideas are your equity, but how you bring them to life is what your focus should be. A big idea is insignificant if you cannot fulfill the promise. Reach high, but start small and manageable. There's always time to do more later.

What follows are information and definitions you will find useful, if not necessary, for devising an idea that will become the product that you will ultimately develop into a venture. However, before you begin the process, it is important to determine your idea's cultural relevance or need, examine the competition, demonstrate how your product will serve the intended audience, and sketch how you will bring it to the marketplace.

THE VENTURE

Let's get our terms straight. The process of developing an entrepreneurial product or business is called a venture. It demands integration of design, aesthetics, craft, business, and marketing. The end product, called the venture, is the culmination of intense research and development made ready for the marketplace or start-up investment.

Begin with what you want your venture to be. Determine its function and role in the marketplace. Develop its form and look. Make it unique through the design and marketing strategies you develop.

A venture can be digital or physical. It can be an object, app, or advocacy campaign. It must be supported with rigorous user-experience research and testing. All assets must be functional. The venture must provide value to an audience that is quantifiable and sustainable.

There are no strict formulae for success, but there are sound procedures for developing a venture. These twelve commonsense steps are recommended during the process of conceiving a product:

1. **Keep a journal** where you put all your random thoughts, formal research, and resources from the onset of a concept. This can take the form of a sketchbook, scrapbook, or online diary. The journal should include notes, doodles, printouts, found

images, and all visual research as well as a meticulous record of all surveys, studies, and resources. Don't be afraid of hoarding notes—as long as you have a system of retrieval, these will come in handy.

2. **Determine "why" and "what."** What is the big idea? Why do you want to do this now?

3. **Identify your audience.** Who cares about this? And why? Define market size and opportunity.

4. **Know your competition.** Who else is targeting your audience? What makes your product different and better?

5. **Get feedback.** From your audience but also from experts—or gatekeepers. Then get more feedback.

6. **Protect your intellectual property.** Apply for a trademark or patent, or copyright your creation so that you have exclusive rights.

7. **Develop your product** and any ancillaries that will help get your audience to the product. Test multiple ideas.

8. **Create a promotion campaign.** Include a short video that tells the product story and defines the key details. Use social media to spread the message.

9. **Identify people to pitch it to:** investors, angels, granting companies, partners, and collaborators. Be prepared to define your product, audience, and purpose. Support your pitch with visuals, prototypes, and timeline.

10. **Develop a product story.** This is your intent, philosophy, and visual strategy. Give examples of how the design direction will convey your message and sell your product.

11. **Create an identity system:** name, logo, and brand.

12. **Define the business model (value exchange).** Give real-world pricing and demonstrate an understanding of production and transition of product to the marketplace.

DECIDING ON THE BEST IDEA, NOT JUST A GOOD IDEA

Designers have plenty of ideas. Ideas are your stock-in-trade. Today, design entrepreneurs are entering a crowded marketplace with ideas that have potential as the basis for unique products. How do you develop and then frame a product that will be valued in either a commercial or social arena?

Thinking is a good way to start. Think about what you would want to use, have, or own. Are there needs you want to address? What would make you satisfied, happy, fulfilled? Every venture has a starting point, and what better place to start than your own experiences? Remember, these are not ends, but instead jumping-off points for transforming the best—not just good—ideas into viable opportunities.

Sometimes, the best ideas result from personal stories, something that you care about and that is important to you. Writing workshop students are routinely told to "write what you know." While it is not a foolproof suggestion, you can conceive an idea based on something you've done, seen, or want to experience.

So, how do you decide which of your ideas to produce or develop so that they turn into successful products, experiences, campaigns, or services? Therein lies the key to a usually difficult door to unlock. Sometimes—indeed often—you are too close to the idea to predict a realistic trajectory. Because you are passionate about the idea, you expect many others to hold the same view. Even if you have captured the hearts and minds of a few people, there's no guarantee your idea will appeal to a sustainable base.

The best idea, therefore, is one that has a likelihood of sustainability. In other words, when your idea is made real, the best one includes a bona fide plan to survive and profit. The ventures that are nonprofit must also be viable. Just as profit must be planned for, the standards and outcomes for nonprofit endeavors must be established before fixating on an idea.

Think of alternatives, too. Everyone has at least one good idea, but that does not limit your scope. Think of variations, complementary and supplementary ideas, that conform to your passions or interests, but be nimble in sketching them out. Often the secondary idea is more viable than the primary.

Let's look at some potential and realized ideas.

The following are MFA Design/Designer as Author + Entrepreneur ventures. They were intensely vetted for viability in order for them to advance to the development stage. Each will provide examples of the thought behind the specific work. You will notice that each has a backstory and narrative structure that serve as the initial rationale for the product. *(Author's note: Developing ventures is occurring at such a fast pace that some of the following may have been produced, discarded, or evolved into other more up-to-date forms by the time this book is published.)*

CASE STUDIES

After Suicide

Bridget Dearborn lost her dad to suicide when she was fourteen. She developed a tool that, through web and mobile platforms, connects people who are dealing with the aftermath of losing a loved one to suicide. While it's not a substitute for traditional forms of therapy, it's designed to provide relief and connection for people who are struggling to find their way.

Lei Lei

Francisco Hernandez, a first-generation Mexican American, created an early childhood educational system that assists Mexican American children in gaining literacy skills while maintaining their cultural identity.

You can be certain that if you are looking for a product or service, other people are looking for the same thing. Your idea can be based on something you need yet are unable to find.

Shared Interest

Chiara Bajardi developed a peer-to-peer lending platform for refinancing student loan debt while she was attending graduate school. Connecting graduates who need access to better interest rates and investors who are looking for more meaningful ways to invest can result in both financial returns and positive social impact.

Likewise, you may own something that has existed for years, but you feel you could do better. Determine how you would improve it and revise and remake.

GreyMatters

GreyMatters is a tablet application by Jenny Rozbruch that improves quality of life for people with dementia and their caregivers. It is a storybook paired with music and games that helps patients and families preserve yesterday's memories.

Or you may simply want to create products that already exist, but you want to add your own voice or personality. Greeting cards, notebooks, textiles: you name it, and if you have a unique idea for a traditional medium, go for it!

North

Donica Ida grew up on a small island in Hawaii, and even though she now lives in a big city, she wanted to help people explore the great outdoors. North is a location-based mobile application that helps people discover nature through the stories of others.

Whatever you choose to do, you must have passion. Time, energy, and resources will be spent, so motivation must be paramount. Once you are certain of your idea, success is in the details.

Rock & Rad

Sylvia Villada wanted to address obesity in children and created a digital book series with animated characters that focuses on healthy eating for children five to eight years old.

In Bounds

Lizzy Showman launched a crowd-fundraising platform that alleviates the financial and social barriers of youth athletics by being a conduit that connects the passion of youth athletes to the hearts of donors.

ESSAY

On the Essence of a Viable Venture

By John Carlin, founder, Red Hot Organization and Funny Garbage

John Carlin is an entrepreneur, art historian, record producer, and cultural historian with degrees in comparative literature from Yale and Columbia University, a Ph.D. from Yale, and a law degree from Columbia. He is the cofounder of The Red Hot Organization, which has produced twenty albums and related television programs, incorporating the talents of leading performers, producers, directors, and visual artists.

ON VIABLE ENTREPRENEURSHIP: When I was trying to wind down a company recently, an interested party needled me by saying it was a shame that I hadn't taken more "value" out of the company. "What do you mean by value?" I asked (knowing he meant money), and then I replied, "I took more value out of the company than I ever expected. I sustained myself economically for many years. And I got to create many innovative creative designs at the dawn of digital culture." He looked at me as if I were crazy.

So, I'm an odd person to ask about the viability of an entrepreneurial venture in a conventional sense. At the same time, I might have a formula that's useful for other creative-minded folk who need to make a living from their labor. For me the essence is a balance of commercial viability and innovative creative opportunity.

That company I mentioned ran for over fifteen years. It participated in and anticipated many of the things we now take for granted in digital culture and modern life: online content, games, social networks, intuitive interfaces, vast enterprise websites, popular mobile applications. We didn't become billionaires, but we affected the way in which digital culture evolved in the first few decades of its existence.

ON APPS AS BUSINESS: I think it's a mistake to think about apps in isolation, just as it was for websites. They are both part of a digital network or system by which people are inventing how to communicate, interact, create, and share content in digital media. Not to mention that apps and websites are essentially the front-end design or UI that often is part of a larger technology infrastructure that supports what we see on a screen.

We are in the early (or prehistory) of digital media, so things continue to evolve and change rapidly. Currently, apps are a great way to engage users and promote a new type of interaction. They also are in the forefront of mobile becoming the primary way people connect with each other and information, as opposed to desktop computers. So apps at present are a great way to create new business models and creative forms of engagement. Just don't think of them as "apps," but as digital delivery systems that are popular for many types of content and interaction that people enjoy and are supported by the first wave of mobile operating systems.

The problem with apps from a business perspective is that they are extremely difficult to market and exist in an increasingly competitive landscape. They are also difficult to maintain from the perspective of content publishing and technology evolution. Responsive websites, which perform very well on mobile devices, remain an effective alternative way to push content, particularly on tablets and large phones.

ON APPS AS AN END IN THEMSELVES: Functionality has been the secret engine of many, if not most, successful digital start-ups and businesses. This was true of early websites, social networks, and now mobile. The essence is to create new, useful, and exciting forms of functionality—that is, better-designed ways to do things. This will probably be true of physical computing and all the ways we interact in the future when we are no longer enslaved to the screen.

ON THE FORMULA FOR A SUCCESSFUL BUSINESS: Again, success is in the eye of the beholder. In commercial terms there are certain formulas one can observe, such as the focus on functionality, utility, and usability I've mentioned in my prior answers.

But there is so much more to success that I would like to see that doesn't fit any formulas—basically, the unknown successes that the future will thank us for. I envision this as new forms of expression and interaction that are intrinsically digital and contemporary, rather than using digital to market and distribute twentieth-century content and concepts. It's a little like saying movies were great in 1914, but they were novelties that paled in comparison with theater or literature. Within decades, movies grew to be one of the great forms of expression in the twentieth century around the world. The ultimate success in and of the digital age will be creative (and business) people who make something new that transforms who we are and how we see the world around us.

ON ORIGINALITY: To be commercially successful, originality is a liability. The folks who come second or third typically are able to improve and capitalize on an idea. Ask the folks at Friendster. Or the people at Xerox Park who gave Steve Jobs and Bill Gates tours of their cool new graphical interfaces.

To be creatively successful, it is important to appear original. Or at least to apply effective ideas from other areas in a new and original way. To use the movie analogy again, the great innovators of cinema such as D. W. Griffith and Sergei Eisenstein both cited Charles Dickens as where they got fundamental ideas such as cross-cutting and the mix of close-ups, medium, and long shots. So their originality was finding something effective in another storytelling medium and applying it to the nascent language of filmmaking. As I often tell students, the important thing is to steal from the right place.

ON TRAITS THAT ENTREPRENEURS NEED: A thick skin. Ha ha! Or functional delusions. I say that because an entrepreneur must be willing to fail. A lot. And keep moving forward based on some odd balance between strategy and opportunism.

Oh, and a creative entrepreneur must have mad visions that the way they see the world is better than all the bigger entrepreneurs out there. You may not "succeed," but it will be a great ride. And to me, that's the greatest success anyone can ever hope for.

SETTING GOALS, WRITING YOUR STORY

Most entrepreneurial ideas start as small concepts and turn into big proposals. The goal is to show how extensive the venture can be and how the creator(s) will go about developing the prototype or final product.

So, now it's your turn:

Your first task is to write a short story about your product.

What is the rationale for it?
What is its history?
What might its future be?

This story is like building the skeleton of a house. On this armature you will put siding, cut in windows and doors, fill it with insulation. This is your foundation.

Now, you may never show your story to anyone, but it can hold the weight of the idea. You might also say it is your blueprint.

Below are some ambitous MFA Design/Designer as Author + Entrepreneur products that derive from personal stories. These two examples began with a simple statement of purpose.

Your second task is to write a statement with your clear goals and expectations. This serves as the first draft of your statement of purpose. Every entrepreneurial project begins with four basic questions that you have to answer:

Why are you doing it?
What is it you are doing?
How are you going to do it?
Who are you doing it for?

CASE STUDIES

Make Manila

Make Manila is dedicated to improving underserved public spaces through community action and transparent fundraising. This web-based platform crowd funds physical pieces of renovation for spaces in Manila. A native of the Philippines, Kara Bermejo wanted to help her city realize its potential and saw her opening for social entrepreneurship in an online community that would encourage direct engagement through financial and material support.

Upacita

Cecil Mariani's Upacita is a business model for arts and cultural organizations and creative indi-viduals in Jakarta to share ownership of collective businesses. It drives revenue to fund projects while aggregating the market power of people. Indonesian-born Mariani also used her emotional ties to guide her decision to create a fundraising project to enhance the cultural life of her city.

WHY

The why of a project is really your belief system. It starts from a very personal story and ultimately will drive the form of the product. It is how you relate to your end user, your audience. You want them to share the same belief as yours, and ideally you want your belief to become their belief too. Hone in on why this particular product is important to you.

To get started, you should write a detailed introduction of the product and why you want to develop it. Explain why you think there is an opportunity in the marketplace to introduce this product and whom it is intended for.

WHAT

Determine what form this idea needs to take and then use design to frame and communicate your concept, eventually turning the concept into a prototype. You will need to identify collaborators, fabricators, developers, and others throughout the process in order to accomplish this. Collaboration is a very important component of being an entrepreneur. Do not think you have to stand alone.

WHO

Identify the target audience for this product. Research what your potential market size may be, and what opportunities exist to reach them. Know what the problems are and state what your solution is. You need to be very clear about what you are offering your audience. What is the value you bring to them? Know what your competition is and show how your unique proposition, solution, and experience is better.

HOW

Identify the gatekeepers in the particular field that your product will live in and get feedback from them. Speak to as many experts as you can. Research and sourcing strengthen the project.

In order to bring an idea to the market, you will have to create a narrative (story), an identity (brand), and a product personality. Also, you will have to be involved with fabricating, marketing, testing, pitching, networking, raising money, and persuading people to come around to your logic.

If you're using social media, make the prototype and launch the product as quickly as possible and iterate with the intended audience. Reassess and fine-tune. Pitch the product to vendors, collaborators, and investors. Develop strategies to promote, launch, fund, and/or sell your product.

You want to maintain ownership of the work you produce, so you must explore legal protection and business practices right from the onset. You must familiarize yourself with intellectual property issues, trademarks, patents, contracts, and other legalities.

ASSUMPTION VERSUS REALITY

Developing your idea involves making assumptions. However, do not rely on these assumptions to reach your goal. These are merely the loose building blocks of a stronger construction—or solid foundation—of facts on which to construct your overall venture.

Nonetheless, these assumptions are a starting point. Based on instinct or reason, experience or conjecture, you may assume that a product or service—an app or object—would be useful to someone somewhere. Or you can honestly say this "thing" is something you would use if it were available. That is your assumption, or let's call it a theory. The next step is to determine that you can make this thing happen: you can design it, promote it, and market it. So far it is blue sky, a wish, a want, a desire. Now go to the next level. Iterate. Sketch it, build it, prototype it, whatever is possible to give it shape and form so that it is no longer sitting alone in your head but can be projected onto others. What you want is feedback from objective critics.

Your first in a series of goals should be to design and develop something of value that can be delivered to an intended audience. Along the way you will be making many assumptions, so do as much research and testing as possible to ensure that these assumptions are correct.

The worst-case scenario is that you embark upon a project only to discover three-quarters of the way through (or even worse, just before launching) that your assumptions were incorrect and it all comes tumbling down. We once had a student spend two semesters developing an improved tool for disabled persons only to learn at thesis review from a critic with the specific disability that the student had based the product on the wrong model. This is where rigorous researching, solid testing, and iterating can make a difference. Do not cut corners. You want to create something that is viable, so you have to know who the potential customer is and how big the potential market can be.

Supposition is not real. Reality is fact. Facts require legwork. This is the stage where you must do the preliminary research to determine the viability and validity of your idea.

Talk to experts in the field. Not just one, but many experts, so you can determine whether you are on the right track.

Get opinions from end users. They will be demonstrative and nuanced in their responses and know if there is true demand.

Scour the marketplace for competitors. Don't just settle for one Google search.

Make certain there is a viable way to fulfill your manufacturing and distribution requisites.

Once you've determined that your offering has potential to viably translate into an actual venture, go back to the drawing board and review and reiterate if you can. Ask questions that haven't been asked. In other words, be critical of yourself. Preempt those questions that might poke holes in your outcomes. Even if you are 99 percent certain, that remaining 1 percent could be a project's undoing. As often as not, as a wise person once said, "the first idea is the best idea." But that means idea, not end product. Refinement is what turns assumptions into reality. Go through the rigors to achieve that refinement.

TRANSFORMING IDEAS INTO ACTIONS

A good idea is nothing without good execution. Good execution is worthless without a firm understanding of how best to realize an idea. Success can be measured in different ways. But at this stage of the entrepreneurial process, success is measured by the ability for making a well-researched concept into a well-realized end product.

Do you want to design a better mousetrap? Or what about a more efficient inhaler for administering asthma medicine? One of our former students, an asthma sufferer, believed from firsthand experience that something better was necessary. He also had a worthy outline for how to achieve this—on the surface. But did this student have the means—not just the talent, but the fundamental ability—to make an efficient device? The answer was no, which did not immediately disqualify the student from proceeding with caution. Frankly, it is possible to find collaborators who have the requisite ability, in this case someone who understands how inhalers work and can oversee production of a prototype. Other business needs, including liability protection, can be addressed after the object is given concrete form. But finding and convincing others of the rightness of the concept was beyond this student's reach within the allotted time frame. Still, it was a beneficial learning exercise. Having the wherewithal to make wishful thinking into a workable prototype is the primary goal at the early stage of entrepreneurship.

This is not an easy goal to achieve. Even Leonardo da Vinci, painter, scientist, and inventor, proposed some forward-thinking inventions, like a flying vehicle that would not have worked even with today's mechanics. But he also proposed machines that were realized centuries later when the technology was available.

Da Vinci serves as a model for the design entrepreneur, for regardless of what the frustrations were, he continued to iterate, iterate, and iterate.

Once the product's form is more concrete, the next goal is to determine where and when it should (or could) be introduced. Decisions have to be made: Does it go directly into the physical marketplace? Does it become the cornerstone of an online community? Does it turn into a campaign, digital app, or other user experience? Do you deliver a service to a targeted audience of like-minded people? Do you put it into the world to see where it finds its audience? A smart entrepreneur does not leave this next essential stage to chance. Even if the product evolves from where it is at this stage, some measure of ownership is required.

This requires identifying the audience and the most likely place for them to access your product. For analog items, there are various options, from traditional mail order to retail merchandizing to online stores, like Etsy or eBay. For digital items, the World Wide Web is a little harder to navigate but nonetheless is an incredible tool. Selling online remains nebulous. For rare or bespoke things, a strategic mention on a well-subscribed blog or Twitter notification or Facebook posting could trigger tremendous response.

Strategic marketing may be as important for the design entrepreneur as actually conceiving and designing the product is. What's more, strategy is an essential ingredient in any serious business plan. Taking action means assuming control of all parts of the overall venture.

Conceiving, fabricating, and marketing the product are not the end, but the beginning of an entrepreneurial journey. Almost all main products can benefit from what we call "ancillaries," which are also collateral materials that help communicate or transmit the product. For instance, when pitching the concept and prototype, it is wise to design leave-behinds that are not throwaways. Where the design entrepreneur lords over the design-challenged entrepreneur is a keen ability to appreciate branded collateral (paper or digital) as a mnemonic or reminder. And it is with branding that the product is giving its heart and soul—even at times with make-believe ones.

Graphic identity frames
the venture in visual and
typographic terms while
the brand tells the story.

CHAPTER TWO

Branding: Creating a Narrative

You've done it for others. Now take the leap and make storytelling part of your own product entity.

Being a design entrepreneur should mean never having to hire a branding firm. Well, probably never. And if you do hire one, at least you know the language of design well enough to speak to the branding designer in a fluent tongue.

IDENTITY AND PRODUCT PERSONALITY

Being a designer means knowing the value of branding and product identity. For instance, you know that in order to succeed, you must create a persona that will attract and inspire your audience. The graphic identity frames the venture in visual and typographical terms while the brand tells the story. Not every product or venture needs to have a public narrative or backstory, but if you choose to create one, make certain it is compellingly plausible.

This process takes shape with a distinct name. It is the first step in the branding process at the MFA Design/Designer as Author + Entrepreneur program. And in the field of "brand naming," Jonathan Bell of Want Branding is an expert; he's worked on over four hundred name creation/consulting projects, invented over fifty company names, and consulted on a significant number of brands, some of which have become household names, including Fruitopia, Citra, Surge, Gillette Mach3, Sirius Satellite Radio, Cingular, Delta Air Lines Business Elite, and more.

Is this a rose by any other name? The truth is, a product is not successful because of its name but because it is a good product. "Would Yahoo and Google have been as successful if they had been named 'WebZone' and 'SearchNet' respectively?" Bell posits. "Probably. However, Yahoo! and Google are great names which have helped to create an aura and mystique and added an intangible component to the brand. These names truly stand out and have helped these firms achieve greater popularity and desirability." Bell insists that great names don't need advertising. "They are advertisements. The iPod, for instance, has quickly reached iconic status and has become the most important product brand in decades."

There are good names, so ergo there are also bad names, such those that are unintelligible, unpronounceable, or pure nonsense. "Ford named an equipment spin-off company Covisint, which is an abomination and has no redeeming qualities whatsoever," Bell warns. "Acronyms are bad unless it's a company that's been around for fifty years, such as GE or IBM."

What about trendy novelty names? Can a major deodorant for men, for example, be called "Bob" or "Stan," and with the right trade character be seen as hip or cool, and therefore desirable? Novelty can be interesting in the short term, yet when pressed, Bell cannot think of a novelty name that has stood the test of time. "Names must have gravitas to secure long-term success," he says.

Before starting a naming project, Bell creates a "Naming Blueprint" which serves as a creative brief for the assignment. It's a way to create parameters for his copywriters so that they eliminate the personal subjectivity inherent in naming. "We also harness our NameBank of ideas," he notes. "This is a database of names from fifteen years of name development. So, for instance, if we're naming a drug which has a rapid onset of action, we can pull up some of our sports car name ideas and maybe get one or two gems from there." Once a short list of names is assembled, Bell's team does preliminary trademark screening in the United States trademarks database to ensure that the names are potentially viable. Google checks are a good way to track whether a name exists and is in use.

At the first presentation, the goal is to find a short list of names that fulfill the "Naming Blueprint" and give the client something to respond to. After that there's a second round of name development, name short-listing, then full trademark checks before a final name is selected. There are certain mandatories in name development, such as "Can you say the name when you see it?" or "Can you say it when you hear it?" Shorter names are better, but there are some famous longer names (Fruit of the Loom). Clients are asked a battery of questions, such as "Do you want a descriptive name like Analog Devices? A real word like Sprint? Or a coined name like Cingular?" There are pros and cons to each name type. Everyone wants a category-defining name, like Kleenex or Hoover, but lawyers hate such names because they can erode trademark protection. For instance, bikini, linoleum, jungle gym, granola, escalator, yo-yo, and zip were all trademarks that became generics.

The desire is for simplicity now. The nineties were definitely about made-up names. Clients want names to have an association and a meaning—names where the client takes a calculated risk and eschews the naysayers. "People have to understand that there's always a negative connotation in every name," says Bell. "Thankfully, David Filo and Jerry Yang ignored the person that said to them, 'You can't name the company Yahoo—it sounds like it's run by a bunch of yahoos.'"

BRAND PLATFORM

An entrepreneur should not be a lone genius (or savant). All aspects of the product, from defining its uniqueness to pinpointing a potential audience, are your responsibility. Where your venture fits into the existing brand environment is useful for many reasons. Creating a visual matrix showing your brand in relation to others positions your product so funders and investors can compare the competition. And it enables you to judge how best to market, promote, and further develop your concept. Here are some examples of the brand platform matrix.

BRAND MATRIX

Knowing where a venture is positioned with respect to similar ventures is useful when creating a brand. The matrix shows whether the space is crowded or free from competition.

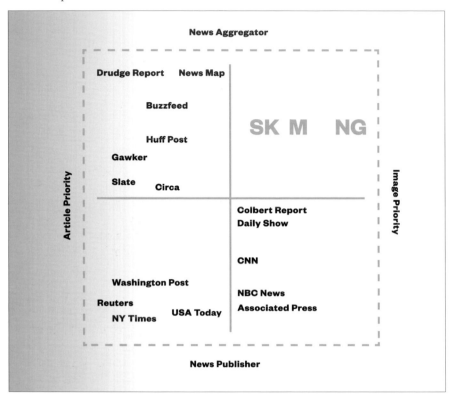

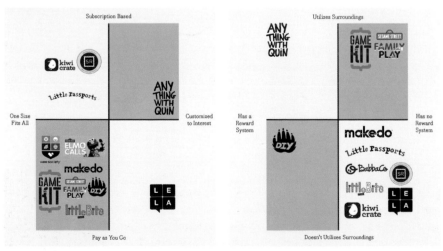

Typical matrices (Top) Positioning SKIMMING an image-based news provider by Kimberly McGuire. (Bottom) Positioning ANYTHING WITH QUIN a parent-child activity game by Diana Haj Amad.

INTERVIEW

A Brand Conversation

KEN CARBONE, PRINCIPAL, CARBONE SMOLAN ASSOCIATES, NY

What is a brand?

Historically, a brand was associated with the name of a commercial product or service. Today, social causes, celebrities, pop stars, athletes, political parties, and even terrorist groups are focused on building their brands. Fundamentally, a brand represents who a company is and what they believe. It is also a promise to deliver a unique customer experience, consistently and reliably, forming a strong emotional bond that increases loyalty.

What is a brand platform?

At the Carbone Smolan Agency, we define a brand platform as an organizational structure that integrates everything a product or service needs to communicate its distinctive qualities and value to key customers. It is the strategy that becomes a trusted road map when launching, refreshing, and maintaining a high-profile brand. It is the synthesis of a name, identity, positioning, messaging, voice (editorial quality and tone), look (graphic applications), and feel (bold, confident, warm, inviting, etc.) as applied across all media.

What does the brand platform do for the entrepreneur?

By nature, entrepreneurs are very intuitive and "go with their gut." This can be effective, but this approach may also lead to inconsistent results that can be costly and time consuming. With an expertly conceived brand platform, the entrepreneur can still optimize all their passion and vision while adding discipline to the brand-building process. The result is a platform that defines what is true and authentic about a brand, what is "ownable" in the competitive landscape, and what value it delivers to a select audience.

How is a design entrepreneur's knowledge of branding best used?

The entrepreneur needs to understand that branding is the sensory presentation and reinforcement of everything a brand promises to deliver. It is much more than "a little logo" because it includes all of the elements in a brand platform. It's how customers interact with a brand in a very real and visceral way, materially and virtually.

CASE STUDY

Nizuc Hotel & Spa:
Where Maya Meets The Twenty-First Century

Nizuc is a luxury beachfront resort and residence on the Mayan Riviera. It incorporates world-class architecture and design, while preserving the natural landscape. It prides itself on delivering a level of service, hospitality, and warmth that redefines luxury. Below is the brand map for Nizuc.

A MEXICAN SPIRIT. A MAYAN SOUL.

A WORLD APART BUT NOT A WORLD AWAY

Once a base station for Mayan astronomers, later a presidential retreat for world leaders, today Nizuc offers a 29-acre private beachfront escape for international travelers, just 15 minutes from Cancun Airport.

MODERN MAYAN

Numerous artistic talents have come together to create a destination that infuses a uniquely modern sensibility with an essentially Mayan ethos — a perfect blend of site specific architecture and design.

ACTIVE RELAXATION

Guests and their families enjoy the resorts multiple pools, six world-class restaurants, two bars and 30,000 square foot spa, to create their own custom vacation experience, ranging from casual conversations with international travellers, sporting activities and excursions to enjoying a moments of solitude contemplating the beauty of nature.

UNTAMED NATURE

Set within a paradise of protected mangroves, and lush local foliage facing the white sands of the Mesoamerican Barrier Reef — the second largest coral reef in the world — Nizuc is home to two private beaches and is surrounded by the regions natural wonders, archeological sites and attractions.

WELCOMING SPIRIT OF FRIENDSHIP AND RESPECT

Nizuc is a place to enjoy the luxe life without the haute attitude. The warmth of the Mexican spirit envelopes each guest upon arrival and extends to every interaction. With each hand-to-heart acknowledgement, guests are reminded of the magical gift that allows them to recapture time, refresh and renew.

Nizuc | Advertising

Nizuc | Identity

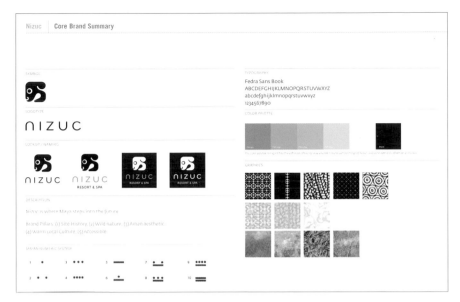

| Nizuc | Core Brand Summary |

TYPOGRAPHY

Fedra Sans Book
ABCDEFGHIJKLMNOPQRSTUVWXYZ
abcdefghijklmnopqrstuvwxyz
1234567890

LOGOTYPE

∩IZUC

COLOR PALETTE

GRAPHICS

LOCKUP / NAMING

∩IZUC   ∩IZUC   ∩IZUC   ∩IZUC
RESORT & SPA   RESORT & SPA   RESORT & SPA

DESCRIPTION

Nizuc is where Maya steps into the future.

Brand Pillars: (1) Site History, (2) Wild nature, (3) Aman aesthetic,
(4) Warm Local Culture, (5) Accessible

MAYAN NUMERIC SYSTEM

| 1 | • | 3 | ••• | 5 | ▬ | 7 | ▬• | 9 | ▬••• |
| 2 | •• | 4 | •••• | 6 | ▬• | 8 | ▬•• | 10 | ▬▬ |

Leslie Smolan, Creative Director
Designers: Wendy Hu, Carla Miller, Daniel Irizarry
Photography: Quentin Bacon

Anatomy of a Brand

At MFA Design/Designer as Author + Entrepreneur, students are required to fulfill an entire brand identity checklist, from logo design to color palette, and then show all the possible applications. The following is the guide the Class of 2014 Graphics Team (led by Timothy Cohan) produced for Venture, the thesis exhibit and pitch presentation. It shows all the necessary assets.

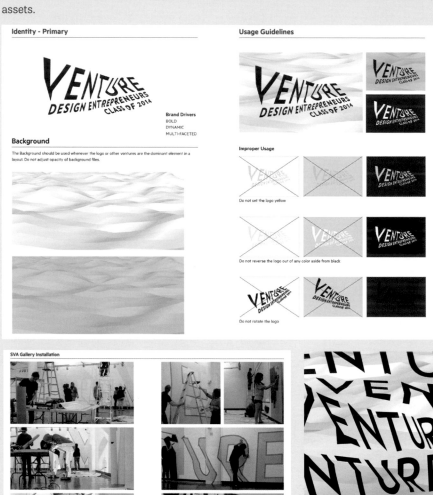

SVA Gallery Elevations and Plan

Venture Website

In addition to a logo and various options regarding usage, a branding manual must show a wide range of storytelling activities and platforms for print, video, and stage.

CHAPTER THREE

Business Models and Sustainable Plans

Y ou need a business plan in order to successfully launch or pitch your product to investors.

In the past, people did not decide to become designers because they were attracted to the nitty gritty of business. Designers begin as artists. Which isn't to say that designers are not good business people. In fact, some are incredibly adept—gifted even—at creating structures and strategies that ensure business sustainability. Anyone who opens a design studio, office, or firm is by definition intimately involved in business. And the business of design is to insure that the work is plentiful, hopefully meaningful, and definitely profitable.

Similarly, design entrepreneurs also have these goals, but a wee bit more is at stake. You are not working for someone (although if you have investors, they are people too) but rather to satisfy your own business needs. Take as much care in developing strategies, schedules, and financial records as you would when dealing with a client.

The following guides by MFA Design faculty members Anthony D'Avella and Zack Yorke focus on the importance of having a viable business plan.

ESSAY

The Design Entrepreneurs' Viability Guide

By Anthony D'Avella, principal, Machine, NY
www.machine.ioh

ESSENTIAL COMPONENTS OF A VIABLE BUSINESS PLAN

When the managers of a business think about viability, they usually think about three related aspects: the long-term prospects of their offer, the amount of revenue they'll be able to generate year after year, and how to optimally manage the business's cost structure as a way to increase profitability (after all, revenue - costs = profit). It's with this profit that the business can invest in growth: the extended marketing of the core offer, hiring new employees, or creating new products or services. (Seed investment and/or venture capital can play the same role of profit in early-stage companies.)

The business plan has traditionally been the way for managers and investors to align on what strategic steps need to be taken to create a viable business. A business plan typically involves assumptions, key stakeholder groups, and near-term actions for managers to execute. But without products or services that first resonate with and later adapt to meet the changing needs of customers, a business plan, whether deemed viable or not, can often be useless if entrepreneurs don't also adapt.

Take a company like Facebook. In 2004, Mark Zuckerberg cared much more about finding users (students at first) that could use his product and help him learn about how to evolve the experience than he did about generating revenue (let alone profit). While the advertising model was eventually integrated into the Facebook experience, that decision was not made until 2008 when Sheryl Sandberg joined the company. And taking a customer-centered product approach has had a distinct impact on how Mark is currently thinking of the experience of ads on the site: "Our goal is to make our ads as interesting and valuable as the organic content that you find on Facebook, to have more people find ads useful so businesses can engage effectively with our community and grow."

You can tell from Facebook's example that a viable business depends on the value it creates, delivers, and evolves with customers, day in and day out. In that way, a business plan should be less a snapshot of perceived success and more of a guide to help managers spot behavioral and market opportunities that are connected, adjacent, or new to the core offer. A good business plan today should be about actions to take, both near-term and in the future, based on the ways customers react both positively and negatively to a business's offer. A business plan is only as good as its ability to help managers continually understand customer needs and integrate that understanding into products and services that generate revenue (and profit) for their business over time.

WAYS TO START THE BUSINESS PLANNING DISCUSSION:

- *Business Model Canvas: www.businessmodelgeneration.com/canvas/bmc*
- *Sequoia Capital (always good to know how investors know a good business plan when they see one): www.sequoiacap.com/grove/posts/6bzx/writing-a-business-plan*

- *I like what Tara Rormor says about not sweating the details at first in this Huffington Post article: http://tiny.cc/brazen-life*

ADVANTAGEOUS COLLABORATIONS

When I think of good collaborations, I think of ways that you can partner with people and companies that can help you push beyond your current capabilities and capacity. So whether it's creating a multidisciplinary group of designers with different skills and perspectives or finding a partner that will help you bring your product to market, the questions are the same: What don't we have that a collaboration might offer? What could someone else contribute that would take longer for us to build ourselves? Quite often, you'll find that the best people or companies that answer those questions will find mutual benefits and valuable ways to grow on their own as a result of the collaboration.

I love Airbnb when I think of a great business collaboration. When people hear Airbnb, they think about the travelers that use their service to book a unique stay in a new city. But when I think of Airbnb, I think about the hosts who own those apartments, houses, or killer spaces that are listed. Without their hosts, Airbnb would not have a business. Plain and simple. For that reason, the company has put incredible time and effort into that collaboration—even sending great photographers to top-rated hosts' homes to shoot their spaces to make them look better—to make sure that hosts feel valued and supported. And that value, trust, and relationship is translated directly back to both travelers, in terms of their experience, and the hosts, in terms of the revenue that they're able to generate. What a beautiful way to build a business with people.

CARRYING OUT A BUSINESS PLAN

1. Intensive roundtable critiques. It's imperative that roundtable discussions and crit sessions include different views from different designers and stakeholders. At our design firm, MACHINE, we say that when you design the product or experience, you're designing the business model at the same time. The point is not compromise, but rather evolution of the product with both the customer and the business needs in mind. The more successful crits of which I've been a part involve product designers providing a rationale for their decisions that unites these two areas.

With those thoughts in mind, I think of four key questions when analyzing the prospects and growth of the overall business:

- *What is our value proposition?*
- *How is the product or experience delivering that value to people?*
- *What is the underlying business model (even if it's just to generate customer engagement at first)?*
- *And (eventually), what capabilities do we need to bring this to market in a continuous way?*

2. Advanced research into feasibility. "What's feasible?" is best answered once your team has an idea on the type of product or experience that you're trying to create. At times, companies will have a unique piece of technology or patented manufacturing process that acts as a source of competitive advantage and a starting point from which to launch product design. And having an idea (as early as the design allows) of what the manufacturing or development might entail can provide crucial input to the design process. But most of the time, and especially with digital products and experiences that are built on open-source platforms, the build analysis and planning depends on what the experience or product design involves.

While I was at IDEO, we designed a new quantified self-fitness tracker for women thirty-five to fifty-four. When we worked out with these women as a way to get inspired, we learned that many of the trackers on the market were okay to wear in the gym, but would never fly on a dinner date. Many trackers were just too bulky or not elegantly designed. Plus, we found that both men and women would often lose the extraneous accessories that came with these devices, like clips, lanyards, or covers. With these insights in mind, we ended up designing a product and sensor set that was small enough to conceal and did not require an accessory. Only when we knew the value we needed to deliver to women did we begin the conversation about how the product should be designed and how feasible it was. And since that moment, the product team has gone through many iterations of the industrial and electrical design, always trying to stay true to the insights that we gleaned from our human-centered research.

3. Refinement and exploration of additional options. Every design entrepreneur should ask themselves, "What's the quickest, cheapest, and easiest way that I can test our value proposition with customers?" Whether that prototype is a piece of paper with a sketch or a set of wireframes with no visual design whatsoever, how can you get reactions from customers (ideally in context with their real behaviors) as a way to guide iteration and generate confidence? Knowing that you're wrong after two weeks of prototyping is far better than finding out you're wrong slowly, painfully, and after a lot of capital (both financial and emotional) has been spent.

4. Defining the market and analyzing the benefits vs. the costs. To me, business is about first defining who your target audience is, understanding their behaviors and needs, describing what problem you want to solve for them, and then detailing the unique value that you're going to create. Market sizing—or understanding how many people are in your target audience—is a crucial step in knowing early on if there is a chance to be successful. Ideally you have to believe that your target market is underserved in some way and that you can capture a large percentage of that group. Even if you capture half of whom you believe you can capture, can you still be successful and profitable?

If you were one of the four founders of Warby Parker, you might have said to yourself, "I think young designers want well-designed glasses for less." Well, how many designers are out there? How much do they spend on average on glasses per year? Multiply those two numbers together and that's your market size. But wait, now that you think of it, maybe other people want well-designed glasses for less. Well, how many more people should we add? The point is that market sizing is part science and part art. How you come to your assumptions will be key to sizing the opportunity that's out there and what your revenue goals should be. For Warby Parker, their market turned out to be most anyone wearing glasses. How awesome is that?

5. Possible redefinition of the product. If you prototype your product and business model with customers throughout the design process, changes to the core offer will happen. Why? Because customer reactions don't happen in your design studio, the classroom, or board room—they happen out in the market with real customers exhibiting real behaviors. What you design should be in direct, iterative response to the inspirational feedback you gather from users on an ongoing basis and from the hunches that your team tests with them.

The key to delivering an exciting pitch presentation is to pitch early, often, and always. Investors and collaborators are not only investing in your idea(s), but they're investing in you—the founder—and your team. Demonstrating knowledge, confidence, and agility in responding to strategic questions are all abilities that only develop over time. Ventures are a work in progress and your audience will know that. How you've thought through their questions in advance and addressed them through your design will gain their attention, respect, and (hopefully) their belief in what you're building. While it might feel scary to pitch your venture in front of people, you'll only address that fear through practice, more practice, and then pitching often.

6. Presenting to Investors

TEAM FIRST
- *Who are you?*
- *Why are you personally passionate (or uniquely qualified) about creating this business?*

MARKET/OPPORTUNITY
- *Who are you serving?*
- *What is their unmet need?*
- *Why is there an opportunity?*
- *How big is that opportunity?*

IDEA
- *Why is your idea unique in the market?*
- *Why is it changing how this customer need or problem is already being addressed?*

RISKS
- *What are the risks? (And be honest, there are always risks.)*
- *How will you address them (if at all)?*

THE ASK
- *How much capital do you need to fund a pilot? The Beta?*
- *In Year 1, what do you believe the costs and revenue will be? What about in Year 5?*

ESSAY

Establishing Value

By Zack Yorke, UX Research and Strategy, Google

Traditional business plans—detailed blueprints for decision making—may be less useful as the world speeds up and becomes less certain. My favorite framework for the essential components of a viable business plan is the one we use to teach our course at SVA's Designer as Entrepreneur MFA Program. First, your brand and value have to show up in the product or experience you create. That's your promise to customers and how you deliver it. Next, both of those drive your business model and capability planning and vice versa. Finally, getting these elements to fit together is an iterative process where you continually turn ideas into tangible next steps. That means getting away from your desk and putting prototypes in front of users to quickly and cheaply test your assumptions. The thinking in your hundred-page document might be sound, but unless you can quickly test your assumptions against the real world, you'll be slow to recognize which part of your plan isn't viable.

Intensive roundtable critique is beneficial, but even better is getting the right kinds of feedback at the right time. Being critical of your next move is great, but you can't let critical rigor get in the way of making a viable product and moving forward.

Advanced research into fabrication is most relevant when the core innovation or user experience is about the material or hardware. Understanding costs has always been essential. But the idea that a designer should know what it takes to fabricate and manufacture is a new and maybe increasingly important thing. We don't really know how important digital fabrication will become, but it's already changing industries, sparking tighter collaborations between designers and engineers, and creating hybrid skill sets.

Knowing your audience is the most important part of building a business. Who do you exist to serve and what makes them tick? What are their needs? How are they meeting those needs now, and what's different about what you bring to the table? How are you going to get their attention, and where do you fit into their day? Research is one of those words that means something different to everyone. Most important is that you have a method to answer your questions. Hopefully that has you talking to users directly, getting prototypes into their hands, and understanding their behavior through data.

Raising money is usually a crucial part of making your idea real, and pitching is the most common way to raise money. But what sometimes gets missed is that you're likely to pitch long before you ask for money. You'll probably do lots of little informal pitches to get friends, family, and collaborators to invest time.

Final refinements and consultation. In a perfect world, all the contributors have quadruple-checked their work, you've gotten sign-off from the boss, and you've tested with the closest thing you've got to real users. All those tough weeks and long hours of prototyping and iteration really pay off here because you've put versions of your product in the wild already. You've "broken" it, made all the necessary repairs, and now you're ready for prime time.

CHAPTER FOUR

Research: Knowing More Than You Know

Simply announcing "my product will appeal to everyone" is only conjecture. Research quantifies all claims one way or the other.

Ever since Google made it relatively simple to answer virtually any question with the click of a mouse, the word "research" has taken on new meaning. Surfing the web does not a priori constitute "proper" research, but it is a step in an essential process. Research is the investigation and acquisition of raw and processed information from various sources—through human contact, close reading, virtual experiences, and raw data. Without research to underscore your strategic plans, your venture is little more than wishful thinking.

The following are research resources and tools that are useful in insuring a greater grasp of your product's viability with your audience.

MARKET TESTING

It will be necessary to gauge the positive, negative, or indifferent response from the prospective consumer. Too often, samplings are conducted with friends or family whose candidness is suspect. By all means get opinions from friends and family, but also test your wares on objective users.

There are various ways to test: individually or in groups, in small gatherings or large events. Find the method that is most conducive to honesty, and establish a format that will produce the best results.

LIBRARY RESEARCH

Nothing beats the library for searching historical precedents. In some cities, like New York, there are business libraries, preserves of untold quantities of valuable records on any number of past ventures. Befriend librarians—they can be great collaborators.

CONSULTATION WITH EXPERTS

Experts are so named because they know—or profess to know—everything about a particular subject. While some experts charge for consultations, others are generous with their time and knowledge if a project strikes their fancy. Finding the expert that best fits your venture's focus may sometimes be difficult, but it's well worth the effort.

ONLINE QUESTIONNAIRES

Questioning a large or small sample of individuals about a potential venture is not the most effective means of collecting data, but it is a start. There are various online services, notably Survey Monkey.

INTERVIEW

Helping Design Entrepreneurs Help Themselves

BEN BLUMENFELD/THE DESIGNER'S FUND

Founded by Ben Blumenfeld and Enrique Allen, The Designer's Fund helps build infrastructure for entrepreneurial opportunities for potential founders and CEOs. They also pair designers with investors and engineers to develop entrepreneurial businesses.

Ben Blumenfeld was a design lead at Facebook for more than five years, where he helped build products for nearly a billion people and grow Facebook's world-class design team. He was also the design director at Varien, which he helped build into one of the world's leading e-commerce firms, and a designer at CBS, where he designed many of their prime-time-show web experiences.

Enrique Allen was a designer at venture capital firms, including five hundred start-ups, Facebook's fbFund, and Venrock, where he helped invest in companies like Wildfire (acquired by Google) and Behance (acquired by Adobe). As a Bay Area native and Stanford University alum, he continues to teach dmedia, one of the most popular courses at the Stanford Design School.

How long has the Designer Fund been in operation?
We incorporated a little over two years ago. The fund is nearly one year old.

What triggered your founding of The Designer's Fund?
We believe the world needs better designed products and services. The fund allows us to invest in the next generation of design leaders and creates a mechanism for successful designers to invest in them as well.

How do you select who and what will be involved?
This depends on the role and how they want to be involved. For example, designers that want to support the next generation of great designer-founded companies are great as Limited Partners for our fund. Designers that are entrepreneurial and want to build those companies are a great fit to be Designer Fund portfolio companies. So, who we select and how they get involved really depends on what they want out of the relationship.

From what we can tell, this is the only such accelerator for just designers. Do you see designers as an untapped resource for entrepreneurship?
We're actually not an accelerator for designers. We see ourselves as building the necessary infrastructure for great designers to build companies with meaningful impact. This means building a great community of designers, investing in them, and supporting them through Bridge, our professional development program for experienced designers.

We do believe design should be brought in at the foundation of building a great company, and more investors and entrepreneurs agree with us. Unfortunately, there

45

is a lack of great designers ready to take that path and knowledge about how to execute design well at this early stage. We hope to change that.

What must a member invest, do, and accomplish while part of the operation?
We don't have members, but depending on your relationship with Designer Fund, there are different expectations. For example, Limited Partners in the fund provide capital and are expected to help companies we invest in from time to time. Advisors, on the other hand, put in more time and are interested in being more active in our community of top designers.

What, in your estimation, makes a potentially successful product?
This is really complex, but if I had to boil it down, we look for something that is addressing a fundamental human need and doing it ten times better than what currently exists. For example, if you compare the Lyft/Uber experience to what was there before—waiting for a taxi, hoping the car is in good shape, fumbling to pay—it's such a better overall experience and addresses our fundamental need to get around.

What are some of the ideas that have come your way?
We really love seeing people bringing design to spaces that haven't traditionally gotten design love. For example, one of the companies we've invested in is Omada Health. They've taken landmark research around diabetes prevention and created a beautifully designed experience around it to prevent people from getting diabetes. The team came out of IDEO's health-care division, so they understand complex system design and making something beautiful and functional. When you compare that to how poorly most health care systems are designed, it makes you really excited for what great design can do.

What are some of your success stories?
It's still early days, but some companies in our fund, like Omada Health, Delighted, and Storehouse, have raised subsequent rounds and are starting to build healthy and sustainable businesses. Additionally, companies we've backed are widely recognized for being design leaders. For example, Storehouse won Apple's Design Award in 2014 for visual storytelling, and Elevate was Apple's iPhone App of the Year. And last, over fifty designers have gone through our professional development program Bridge and are now working at some of the top start-ups in San Francisco, including Airbnb, Dropbox, and Pinterest.

Indeed, what is success in your terms?
We want to look back ten years from now and see that we had an active role in helping build companies that build products and services with great design and an active role in creating the next generation of design leaders.

This appears to be the age of design entrepreneurship. What have you noticed that has changed in the past couple of years amongst this group?
More and more designers are seeing entrepreneurship as a path they want to take but are uncertain about how to do it well. The flipside is that more great engineers, busi-

ness leaders, and investors want to build great design into their companies but are uncertain about how to execute that at a high level. So the past couple of years have seen
a big increase in the demand for design entrepreneurship, but meeting that demand
has been a real challenge for everyone involved. We'll believe we'll get there—it'll just
take a concerted effort from everyone involved. The great news is the result will be a
world where we see beautifully designed products and services all around us.

What does the future (next year) look like in your world?
We hope to continue to invest in great designer cofounded companies, help develop
the next generation of great design leaders through Bridge, and build the infrastructure for designers everywhere to take the path of entrepreneurship.

Big Research Questions

BENJAMIN GADBAW, DESIGNER, IDEO

What is essential about research in entrepreneurial pursuits?
Research provides the connective tissue between an entrepreneur's unrelenting desire to bring something into the world and the unmet needs and aspirations of the world's population. In my opinion, without research, entrepreneurship is more like art or invention without application. Depending on the entrepreneur and the pursuit, research may help find the right customer, adjust the story about the product so that it resonates with an audience, or prioritize an entrepreneur's energy to create a near-term experience worth launching that maintains a trajectory toward a larger vision. In all of these cases, research connects the idea with the need.

Research for design inspiration is done when designers feel motivated to create. Fundamentally, research can generate new ways of thinking that are inaccessible when a designer is simply sitting in front of a computer. Research to a designer can be like stream-of-consciousness writing for a novelist—research can break through designer's block. In that sense, research can never be overdone, because it is a mindset more than an activity. It's having curiosity about people and the systems they live in; it is putting a question mark on strongly held beliefs.

Sometimes research is much more tactical; it means an entrepreneur has a great product but customers are behaving unexpectedly. For example, they are adding products to a cart but completing checkout only 10 percent of the time. Analytics can reveal where in the customer journey the unexpected happens. But why is that? Maybe they are using the cart to bookmark without any intention of purchasing. Maybe there is a social, emotional, or cultural reason. Stepping back from the product can shed light on why a behavior is happening.

The purpose of research is to provide velocity to a design project. So if an entrepreneur is moving forward in the right direction, they have done their due diligence, but as their product, competition, society, and technology evolve, so does the right velocity. If entrepreneurship is a sailboat, research is the rudder.

Is it necessary to do ethnographic research or does any "market test" fit the bill?
Ethnographic research is unique. I cannot fairly say that it is necessary in all situations. It depends. In market research, there is sometimes an over-reliance and a misuse of surveys that misguide would-be entrepreneurs. People don't always do what they say they do, they don't do what you think they do, and they don't do what *they* think they do! Ethnography uncovers latent needs that people do not articulate.

How does one best present research findings?
The best way to present research findings is to avoid the situation of presenting research findings altogether. When people observe firsthand the experience of who they are designing for, they are more compelled to think differently about those people and how to design solutions for them. So whenever possible, include everyone on the team in research as early and as often as possible. Unfortunately, this is not always possible.

A pitch can be as simple as a short conversation or a sketch on a napkin. It can also be a choreographed presentation.

CHAPTER FIVE

Pitch and Presentation

Getting investors, angels, collaborators, and accelerators interested in a venture requires both effective design and smart stagecraft. As an entrepreneur you must be ready to engage, enlighten, and seduce those who are necessary to making your venture a reality, not to mention a success.

MAKING THE PITCH

When you are ready to tell your story, you will have fine-tuned your "pitch." Under this rubric is an ensemble of materials and performances that will, at the very least, pique your target's interest or excite them enough to commit to investing. Pitching has become more elaborate since access to video production and other digital tools is so easy. Kickstarter has both raised the bar and lowered the entrance requirements for entrepreneurs to present their concepts. The ability to crowd fund has opened the entrepreneurial playing field, but has also made it virtually unacceptable to do something amateurish.

A pitch can, however, be as simple as a short conversation or a sketch on a napkin. It can also be as complex as a choreographed presentation with bells and whistles. It all depends on the "stakes" in play. Although a small idea could become a huge venture, usually the modest pitches have just as much impact as the ambitious ones if handled with skill and talent.

VIDEO

Video has been a real boon in the pitch and presentation process. With skilled editing and high (though modest) production values, which are at everyone's fingertips, your presentation can be "pitch perfect." Video editing allows the entrepreneur to make different versions for different audiences, as well as update and refine content based on responses from those audiences.

The most effective pitch videos are, however, teasers for a more detailed presentation. They are the video equivalent of the "elevator pitch," that is, a pitch that is completed in the time it takes to rise or descend in an elevator. Videos are complements to the "dog and pony" presentation.

WATCH IT GROW

IDEA

ONE IDEA AT A TIME

REAL

THE WORD

BoCo

Two examples of video pitches. BoCo (above) by Jose Fresneda is a proposal for a crowd-sourced design advice and advocacy organization in Colombia. It is simple, graphic, hand designed to show that it is an idea whose time has come. Pincil (below) by Timothy Cohan is an online sketch gallery for passionate drawers to share their work with others.

Made Here by Justin Colt reinvents how products are manufactured and sold, enabling designers to manufacture product ideas and sell to retailers.

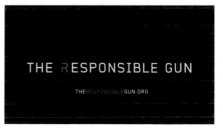

The Responsible Gun by Thai Truong is not a typical venture, but a pitch for an organization "determined to find a middle ground between gun rights and gun control groups through the development of responsible ideas and technologies." The video is an artful polemic against irresponsible gun use.

Catco by Yiming Bao is an online community for creative people to experiment with art and technology —and promotes collaboration. Using easy-to-read images, the video reveals the informal, witty, and handmade essence of the venture.

DOG AND PONY

The reference to dog and pony derives from old carnivals where the usually cute dog and pony shows on the midway attracted awestruck kids. In terms of entrepreneurial presentation, a dog and pony show should have more gravity. In fact, it is a performance that shows your ability to personally engage with your audience and convincingly celebrate the virtue and value of your venture.

These presentations come in many configurations. They can be an intimate gathering of one or two people, or larger audiences, where you may literally be on stage. Every week, at most accelerators, developers present before rooms of people. It's a highly admired skill to do these right. Which is why seeking professional consultation is a good idea.

In the MFA Design/Designer as Author + Entrepreneur program, a six-week class is set aside for instruction with a theatrical coach who choreographs, rehearses, and trains students on how to speak, stand, and otherwise comport on a stage in front of an audience. These lessons are valuable not only for entrepreneurship but also for professional life in general.

Remember...

Pitching is not just an impromptu talk: it is the strategically coordinated (and often scripted) acts of a play designed to persuade the audience that what you have to offer is unique and potentially successful. There are many steps to follow below.

Now, on with the show...

CHECKLIST FOR YOUR PITCH

Before creating a pitch presentation or making a pitch to investors or partners, consider the following questions as necessary in a proper proposal:

UMBRELLA TOPIC
  What's the big idea?

CULTURAL RELEVANCE
  What does the world need?
  Why now?

AUDIENCE PROFILE
  Who cares? And why?
  For whom are we creating value?

COMPETITIVE OVERVIEW/CORE COMPETENCY/
BRAND CHARACTERISTICS
  Who else is working with your audience?
  What makes your product special?

53

DESIGN DRIVERS/VISUAL RESEARCH
What might it look like?

PRODUCT SKETCHES
Overview of two to four idea explorations

PRODUCT FOCUS
Walkthrough of most current iteration

BUSINESS MODEL
What are the most important costs?
How do we make money?

RESEARCH
Documented feedback from your audience (and your "key people")
What future research will you undertake—ethnography, articles, books?

NEXT STEPS
What are the next five steps to make it real?

HOW TO PITCH

There are different ways of interesting an investor or partner in a venture, but the key is professional discipline. Here is a general template for how to present and comport yourself in a formal pitch. It works for an informal one too.

INTRODUCE YOURSELF
- *State your name and project name.*
- *Introduce your venture.*
- *Define product, audience, and purpose.*

EXPLAIN YOUR GOALS BY BREAKING DOWN YOUR
- *Research*
- *Audience*
- *Competition*
- *Cultural relevance*
- *Business model*
- *Market size and potential*

VISUALLY PRESENT YOUR VENTURE
- *Prototypes*
- *Sketches*
- *Diagrams*
- *Any relevant graphic material*
- *Initial branding*

DEFINE NEXT STEPS
- *Advisory board and current partners*
- *Timeline for fabrication, marketing, testing*

REMEMBER TO
- *Describe rules of the road.*
- *Talk directly to your audience.*
- *Be confident and persuasive.*
- *Stay on topic; do not go off on tangents.*
- *Use Keynote or another effective presentation tool.*

PITCH KEYNOTE OR PROPOSAL BOOKS

The suggested medium for a pitch is Keynote or another presentation tool, but you should leave behind a document covering the same ground in more detail. A fully designed proposal book or PDF is recommended. (There are many services that will bind and laser print such a book.) The following content is essential to include in your book.

YOUR NAME

VENTURE NAME

TABLE OF CONTENTS

EXECUTIVE SUMMARY
Two sentences, max

PRODUCT DEFINITION AND PURPOSE
Detailed description of product
(include detailed prototype sketches or renderings)

VISUAL STRATEGY
Explain how the design direction will convey your message.

DRAFT OF THE IDENTITY SYSTEM
Name, Logo, Type, Color, Illustration, Photography, Patterns, etc.

CULTURAL RELEVANCE AND AUDIENCE
How the end user discovers and uses the outcome
What was learned from customer testing

COMPETITION
Discuss how the venture better addresses the audience.
Define market size and opportunity.

BUSINESS
Define the business model (value exchange).

BIBLIOGRAPHY
List all resources, documentation, and online research according to MLA style.

The pitch for InBounds by Elizabeth Showman, a crowd-funding platform to alleviate "the financial and social barriers of youth athletics," packs a double wallop. First she plants seeds of interest with a video that is clear and engaging, then in the pitchbook all the details are clearly arranged for the large and small donor.

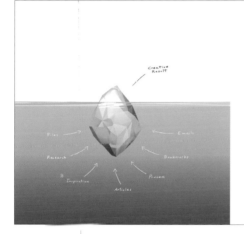

Iceber.gs

An innovative organization app for creative minds.

Icebergs is a web application that lets you collect, filter and connect your inspiration and projects like never before. Internet research, notes, files and emails in one single place. A revolutionary human approach to how creative professionals and students organize themselves. Icebergs it's been designed to turn your working life into a completely new experience.

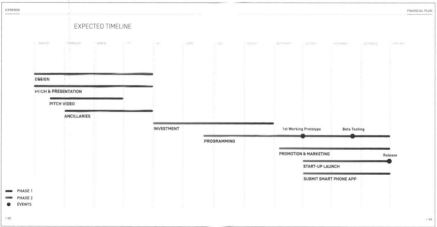

Pitchbooks are printed documents but they can also be "decks" or slide presentations. This for Iceber.gs by Albert Pereta was created as an organization app "to help creative minds collect, explore and connect" their projects in one place. The book shows the development of the idea through to the business plan.

PRODUCT STORY

Last summer I rediscovered my passion for drawing in Rome. The city smashed a creative block and inspired me to get my hands dirty. Inspiration struck one afternoon on a walk through the center of the city. I found a café across from the Pantheon and stared up at the towering structure for a few moments.

App: Submit a sketch

Public Advertising

The advertising and marketing program is important in the early phases of *Pincil*. In addition online marketing which is low cost, having a presence in the physical urban environment would be powerful. It could help define "hot spots" for artists to draw and in the process build pockets of density in the collection. Locations should be highly visible and above ground so that people can access the Internet on the spot if desired.

Timothy Cohan's pitchbook for Pincil, designed to feel like an analog version of a smartphone, gives the product story as well as options for advertising and promotion. It compels the potential user to draw and draw.

MADE HERE IS A PLATFORM FOR DESIGNERS TO CONNECT WITH MANUFACTURERS & RETAILERS TO TAKE PRODUCT IDEAS FROM CONCEPT TO RETAIL SHELF.

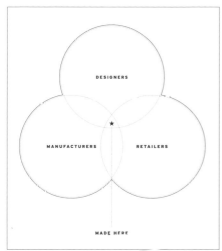

Made Here by Justin Colt "reinvents how products are manufactaured and sold." It makes it easy for makers to build and sell their products online by connecting with their vendors and manufacturers. Here is shown the space that Made Here would occupy.

Funnelcake is an iPad game that ignites curiosity.

Through rich visual experiences, Funnelcake lets kids tinker with scientific concepts.

Cultural relevance

We're in a time when scientific discoveries and technological advancements are happening at a record pace. And these findings, these inventions are each the products of those who are as curious about the world as I am

Investing in science education is really about investing in our future. Only 5% U.S. workers are in science and engineering, yet those jobs provide more than 50% of the countries economic expansion and growth.

At the moment there are 2-3 million unfilled technical positions that are estimated to rise to 10 million by the end of the decade. (NYSCI, "Design, Make, Play.")

But why are so few Americans working in the field of science and engineering? In early 2009 the National Assessment of Educational Progress found that only 30% of 8th graders and 21% of 12th graders were proficient in Science.

> "Kids don't feel connected to what they are learning."
> — Barry Fishman Professor, School of Education University of Michigan

Last year the Organization for Economic Cooperation and Development (OECD 2013), release the PISA 2012 Results: "What Students Know and Can Do = Student Performance in Mathematics, Reading and Science" (Volume I), 15 year olds in the United States performed below average in science and didn't do any better on their math and reading scores. 27 countries performed better than the United Stated and among them; Shanghai, Hong Kong, Singapore, Japan, Finland, Korea, Canada, Poland, the Netherlands and Switzerland.

Recently programs have been developed to revitalizing interest in these subjects. The Google Science Fair is one, an online science competition

The application

Funnelcake by Simone Noronha is a game for the iPad that "ignites curiosity." To attract interest the pitchbook shows the lighthearted graphic idenity combined with the engaging scientific content.

Announcing the Password → Stalls

In addition to the password announcement on facebook, a sticker campaign was launched in the bathroom stalls, starting at the American University of Beirut. The stickers were pasted in the girls' stalls as well as around the sink and soap areas and featured the Beinetna bubble with the URL and password. This technique sets well for the first launch, but the future passwords will be updated weekly on the facebook group.

Promotional Video

The Beinetna launch video was launched on the facebook page and clicked around social media with the aim to get the name out before launching the website. The video is a mix of live action footage of a girl in a bathroom stall and after effects typographic animation of conversations appearing on the walls of a bathroom stall. The final scene writes "Don't you wish we could talk about this outside these walls?", and cuts to a scene of the stall covered in handwriting, delivering the message that there is an alternative space for having conversations like these, and that space is beinetna.com.

Beinetna by Leen Sadder is conceived to be an initiative in Bierut, Lebanon, "dedicated to eliminating the stigma surrounding women's health and sexuality." The pitchbook helped to position the need for this and show how these socially taboo ideas can be communicated online.

Personal History

My personal experience with dementia comes from caring for my grandmother, Frieda, who is now 91 years old. Due to her advanced vascular dementia, she is unable to perform daily functions on her own, and receives full-time care from my family and her home Medicaid aides. Although Frieda's short-term memory is gone, and her physical mobility is limited, she still finds joy in companionship and cognitive stimulation. I have witnessed how her spirit and long term memory can be drawn out dramatically through activities like listening to music from her youth, looking through old family photos, and hearing her life story told back to her. It's amazing to see how much her mood and manner change when she is simply engaged. Some of the best moments we've had together in recent years have occurred while listening to Frieda's favorite songs. I am always in awe watching her sing along with clarity, as lyrics seem to magically return to her mind.

But the overall realities of dementia are not easy to bear. As my grandmother's condition has progressed over the past six

Product Description

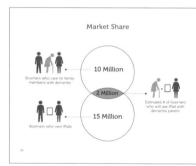

GreyMatters is a tablet application that aims to improve quality of life for dementia patients and their caregivers. Through cognitive and sensory engagement, GreyMatters helps to foster feelings of self-worth and delight for people with dementia, and strengthens their connections with loved ones. With a strong belief that people with dementia are "still here," GreyMatters taps into the abilities that remain to keep individuals engaged and connected.

The iPad app offers personalized sensory stimulation through simple tools such as a life storybook, music and memory games—all with the ability to customize content using photo and voice note uploads. These reminiscence activities evoke an individual's life story, allowing the person with dementia to access memories and functioning that still remain, but are difficult to tap into without help. In addition to reflecting on the past, it allows patients and families to create and share new moments together. The app also functions as a calming tool in times of anxiety or agitation.

Market Share

10 Million — Boomers who care for family members with dementia

2 Million

15 Million — Boomers who own iPads

Estimated # of boomers who will use iPad with dementia patient

Business/Financials

There are currently 15 million Americans who provide unpaid care to a parent or other family member with dementia.[1] Many of these individuals are baby boomers (ages 48 to 66), who currently control about three fourths of America's wealth. These boomers are also tech savvy and spend a great deal of time online, particularly for health reasons.

PRICING & VENUE
The GreyMatters app will be sold through the iTunes store for approximately $19.99, with in-app purchases ranging from $0.99-$2.99. In-app purchases will be extremely valuable to the GreyMatters experience, as they will include content packs that are personally significant to the patient. For example, if an individual seems to respond best to photos of babies, a caregiver could download a collection of related photos that have been curated specifically for this audience. These content packs will be available through individual download, or through a yearly content subscription, priced at $9.99/year.

VISUAL INSPIRATION — Vintage Photo Albums

VISUAL INSPIRATION — Unique Imprints in Body and Nature

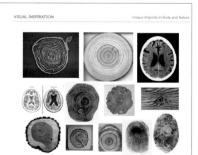

Greymatters by Jennifer Rozbruch is a tablet application that hopes to improve the quality of the elderly with dementia and their caregivers. The video shows the human essence while the pitchbook is like a guidebook on how this app works.

CHAPTER SIX

Funding: Seeding the Venture

Design entrepreneurship is often an investment of time and energy but also initially paid for out of pocket by the designer. If you are committed to the venture, it makes sense to get it off the ground in any way possible. Nonetheless it is important (and wise) to explore other funding options.

OPTIONS

VENTURE CAPITAL

Venture capital (VC) is the name given to funds invested in early-stage start-up businesses. Venture capital fund groups such as Kleiner Perkins Caufield & Byers identify potential growth companies that require funds when the initial seed round expires. Returns on investments are expected if and when the company is sold or becomes a publically held entity.

ANGEL INVESTOR

An angel investor provides capital for a business start-up, in exchange for equity in the venture. Angels can be either individuals or organized networks who pool their resources. Angels act as mentors and consultants to their "portfolio companies."

ACCELERATORS

Start up accelerator programs are industry-focused programs centered on fashion, food, and socially conscious endeavors as well. Most provide funding, mentorship, and access to potential investors. However, accelerators are not a magic carpet ride. It is important to understand what these programs are able to achieve. For some they are golden, for others, well . . .

CROWD FUNDING

This area of investment has exploded in recent years, allowing low-intensity investment in heartfelt projects.

The Art and Science of Setting Kickstarter Goals

By Steve Kroeter, founder, Designers & Books

Kickstarter is an efficient, cost-effective, and inspiring tool for crowd funding your creative project. Its premise is simple: you determine how much money you need to realize your project, and you mount a campaign for that amount for a fixed period of time on the Kickstarter website. "Backers" go to the website and pledge dollars (via credit card) to support your project. For their support, backers receive customized rewards that you offer as an incentive to engage. How elaborate the reward is depends on how much is pledged. You can create various tiers of rewards. Unlike some crowd funding ventures, Kickstarter is all or nothing. If you raise enough money to reach or exceed your stated funding goal, the backers' credit cards are charged and you get the money. If you don't meet your goal, you don't get any funds at all.

One of the keys to getting funded on Kickstarter is to choose a strategically and financially sound funding goal. While the beauty of Kickstarter is that you don't incur the major costs of implementing your project until you actually have the funds to do so, there are costs, of course, associated with putting together and running the Kickstarter campaign itself. You'll want to account for those in addition to your project costs.

Getting your goal amount right involves combining numbers—some that can definitively be determined and others that can only be estimated. For first-timers, this duality can cause a bit of a dilemma. Where do you start the process, given that you know some numbers but have to guess at others? And how do you bring those calculations together in a way that favors getting funded, that covers all your true costs, and that allows you to optimally realize your project?

At Designers & Books, we are using Kickstarter for a series of publishing projects focused on books about design. Although the specifics would have to change to fit your particular project, the thinking behind the approach to one of our book projects can be used as a model for almost any Kickstarter project. Kickstarter encourages personality, creativity, and fun as you pitch your project and connect with backers. However, since money is on the line, a carefully thought-out and systematic approach can be helpful in establishing your funding goal.

When beginning the goal-setting process, it's helpful to imagine what the end result looks like—which means understanding your goal in relation to the overall expense structure associated with it. Use a spreadsheet to keep track of all your costs. This gives you an easy way to stay aware of what you'll actually have available after deducting not only the costs specific to your project (your fixed and variable costs), but also the fees associated with getting funded, which can amount to 10 percent or more of your funding goal amount.

The costs that are specific to your project can be divided into two types: fixed costs and variable costs.

FIXED COSTS

Fixed costs don't change over the course of your Kickstarter campaign—meaning they stay the same regardless of the number of backers you get or the amount of money pledged to your project. Examples of these types of costs are:

- *For a book, fixed costs include writing, editing, design, and—for a set number of copies—printing and production*
- *Campaign costs include:*
  - *Production of the video on Kickstarter that introduces your project to potential backers (This is a must.)*
  - *Setting up your Kickstarter page*
  - *Promotion and audience engagement before, during, and after the course of your campaign—including press releases, social media messaging, and implementing an email campaign*
  - *Incorporating your Kickstarter campaign into your website or blog, or setting these up if you don't have them already*

Whether you get 500 or 1,000 or 2,000 backers, these costs don't change.

VARIABLE COSTS

Variable costs involve aspects of your Kickstarter campaign that are impossible to predict and that you will know for sure only when your campaign is over. They are related to how you structure the rewards to your backers—for example, how many reward tiers you offer and how each individual tier is designed and priced. There's no way to know in advance how many backers you are going to find or how the backers you do find will be distributed over your reward tiers.

Depending on what your rewards are, the key variable costs are:

- *The manufacturing cost of the rewards. In the case of a book, the end product or some version of it is frequently the reward (an advance page proof or a finished copy, for example), so these can be counted as fixed costs. But any part of a reward tier that's not produced as part of the project itself should be accounted for.*
- *Fulfillment costs of the rewards, e.g., the costs of shrink-wrap or other packaging of the rewards, the cost of assembling the rewards into the mailing materials, and the cost of the mailing envelopes or boxes*
- *Domestic and international shipping costs of the rewards*

To get an understanding of the fulfillment and shipping costs and how to account for them, you'll have to make some assumptions about the number of backers you think you can attract to your project, and at what reward tier they will pledge. You can then create different scenarios based on those assumptions.

You can approach developing an estimate of backers in several ways.

- *Research the number of backers that similar projects on Kickstarter have attracted.*
- *Assess the size of the audience that you think will find out about your project based on your online presence and personal connections.*

Once you have experimented with a range of backer scenarios at different goal levels, you can consider the average pledge per backer for similar projects on Kickstarter. Dividing your goal by the average pledge per backer will give you another possible indication of the number of backers you might be able to attract.

At this point, if you are using a spreadsheet, your work will include rows of reward tier options—with a projected number of backers associated with each tier. If you will be offering your rewards internationally, then the projected number of backers has to be divided into a "domestic" component and an "international" component.

For fulfillment costs, you can (on your own or with the help of a fulfillment center) estimate the "per unit" cost of packaging, assembly, and mailing materials costs for each of your reward tiers. You can then do the same with shipping costs, creating a "per unit" cost of shipping for each of your reward tiers for each region (national and international) you will ship to.

The assumptions for your variable cost components outlined here—reward tiers, the number of backers, the distribution of backers by tier, and the distribution of backers by domestic and international ship-to addresses—along with your fulfillment and shipping costs provide you with all the elements you need to consider, via a spreadsheet, the impact of different scenarios.

CAMPAIGN FEES

Mounting a Kickstarter campaign entails fees that are "fixed" in the sense that they are a percentage of total funds raised, but variable in the sense that they are a function of the amount you raise.

These fees include:

- *Kickstarter's fee of 5 percent*
- *Credit card processing fees, usually anywhere from 3 percent to 5 percent (Kickstarter now uses Stripe for credit card processing)*

You will want to provide for credit card pledges that might not successfully process. Some estimate this amount at 1 percent of total funds raised.

As is always the case in business, unforeseen circumstances can arise and throw off even the best planning practices—a rise in shipping rates, lost shipments that need to be replaced, and so on. For this reason, it is a good idea to add in a contingency factor. A figure frequently used is 5 percent.

At this point you can begin to identify, for various scenarios you choose, the minimum amount necessary to fund your project—which is one way to think about the amount of your Kickstarter goal. In your spreadsheet, you can calculate the amount you will earn from all your pledges, based on the assumptions about the number of backers you think you will attract to each of your reward tiers and the price associated with each tier. From that amount you can subtract:

- *Fixed costs*
- *Variable costs associated with your backer and reward structure scenarios, including fulfillment and shipping*
- *5 percent for the Kickstarter fee*

- *5 percent for the Stripe fee*
- *1 percent for failed credit card processing*
- *5 percent for the contingency*

After doing the above subtractions, if your result is greater than $0, based on your assumptions, you are in what we might call "tentative break-even territory." If your result is less than $0, you might want to review the assumptions about your costs and rewards structure.

Some entrepreneurs, given the vagaries of the business environment and having identified the tentative break-even territory, will take a conservative approach and add a cushion amount to the funding goal.

Others, for various reasons, might decide to be more assertive. For example, an often cited Kickstarter-related metric* is that "90 percent of the campaigns that reach 30 percent of their funding goal in the first week get funded." This inserts yet another variable into the mix of determining your goal—your willingness to consider a somewhat lower goal to motivate backers to pledge sooner rather than later and thereby help you reach that 30 percent tipping point sooner rather than later.

That counts as one more factor in the art and science of determining how to decide the Kickstarter goal amount that's right for your project.

A note of thanks to Rachel Presser of Himalaya Studios, Christopher Hawker of Trident Design, and George Rohak of Breadpig for their helpful comments on the topics addressed here.

* www.entrepreneursthatsoar.com/blog/getting-started-with-crowdfunding

The Serial Investor

LINDA HOLLIDAY, FOUNDER, CITIA

How do you define "angel" investing? What are its distinguishing features? And in what ways, if any, does it differ from venture-capital investing?

Angels are amateurs and VCs are professionals—meaning that they have raised funds from outside partners and are running an organization that vets and manages investments. Angels are often acting as individuals, and VCs are really committees. Angels have very few rights, VCs have more. Many VCs do angel investing as individuals as well.

It's my experience that angels are a little more emotional, and they get connected to ideas and entrepreneurs. VCs at least try to make more financially driven decisions. I actually have my own mantra as an angel: I don't want to invest in anything I don't want to pay attention to! You'll be with these companies probably for several years, for follow-on rounds and business hurdles. It really helps if you are intellectually engaged with the business. Also, sometimes you just fall for an entrepreneur—more as a coach or a mentor. It can be very satisfying to help them through some of the inevitable challenges and to watch them succeed.

Unfortunately, both groups of investors can be very trend driven, always looking for the next Pinterest or Uber. That makes it much easier to get an iterative idea funded than an original one.

How do you become and angel and how do angels work?

You need to be an accredited investor (assets of $1 million not including primary residence or more than $200,000 a year in income).

All you have to do is call yourself an angel and make at least one investment. You can also join groups like the New York Angels. Some people do this very professionally, as a career. Other people only invest in people they know; other people do any other set of things you can imagine! Being good at it is another story.

At what stage of a company's life cycle is it most advisable to approach an angel investor? Can it ever be too soon or too late for an angel?

Unfortunately, as the options for early financing increase with platforms such as Kickstarter, and the competition for seed money gets more and more intense, most angels now want quite a bit of "de-risking" before investing. So, that often means that the product has been built and/or tested with some users. It's usually too late to approach an angel only if you've already pushed the valuation for the company beyond seed level (3–8 mm pre-money, the value of a company before investment). Even that is flexible and changing. You should definitely have a good team together, and enough assets so you can convince strangers that you can pull something off. When I teach my class on entrepreneurship, the first day I come in I ask the students to give me $1,000. That kind of makes the point.

Is angel investment more advantageous than borrowing as the means for a company to finance growth? Why or why not?

It's extremely difficult to obtain debt financing for seed companies. But if you can get it, it would prevent significant dilution. I learned business the old-fashioned way—that selling equity was very expensive; that you should do everything you can to hold equity. Alternatively, given the high failure rate for start-ups, many entrepreneurs might be nervous to finance significantly with debt.

Many entrepreneurs are relatively inexperienced, and if they have the commitment of some experienced angels, it can make a big difference in whether they succeed or fail. In an ideal world with lots of choices, angels would be selected for that experience.

What have you found to be some of the more common misconceptions held—or mistakes made—among entrepreneurs who seek angel investor support?

Most entrepreneurs are shocked to find out just how much of their company they have to give away to raise angel funds. If you look at the investment class and do the math, if one third to one half of the companies fail and one half of the remainder are essentially flat, the last portion has to generate a huge multiple for an investor to break even. It's not uncommon for an angel to be looking for a ten-times or greater multiple on their investment. Of course, that doesn't mean they get it.

It really is a buyer's market for investors. Entrepreneurs will only have one shot at an investor. You really have to have everything buttoned up. Everything. And unfortunately, that often means having a serial entrepreneur with a successful exit on the core team. It's the greatest predictor of success.

For me, I look for domain expertise or at least the fact that a lot of research has been done. We're in a moment now where having no experience is somehow seen as a disruptive advantage. Wake me when it's over!

What tools or metrics have you found to be the most reliable means of evaluating a company's investment worthiness? What would you consider the three most critical characteristics of an investment-worthy venture?

It's hard to trust metrics too much, since really all you're buying is a story that happens in the future. Some metrics, like referrals or time spent with the product, can have strong predictive value, though.

When evaluating an entrepreneur I like to ask myself the question, "Would I hire this person to run, say, a $10 million department? For five years? Unsupervised?" That's the level of confidence you need to have in somebody. For me, that clears things up pretty fast.

Three important investability characteristics would be:

• *An idea that's riding one or more important tech trends*
• *An entrepreneur who is plausible, with a well-considered game plan . . .*
• *In an area that I would consider myself qualified to evaluate.*

Are there any particular business sectors, scenarios, or needs for which you feel angel investment is best suited?

There are many ways to be an angel investor. The tech sector is obviously very hot—so is e-commerce. Being an angel in those areas could lead to a vibrant professional life. You may also want to stay close to the industries you understand most or are interested in most. Many angel investments will require follow-on rounds. It's a good idea to think about what the life cycle for the company is and whether or not you have the patience, or as we say, the "powder" for it. Many angels are looking for investments that will exit relatively quickly. (A $2 million valuation now for a $20 million exit in two years is one desirable formula.) Other angels are looking for a "Hollywood hit" and want to make many bets. If the sector you're looking at doesn't have a history of raising follow-on rounds of investments, it's probably too risky as an angel, unless you think that company can get to break-even on seed money.

Do you feel that there's value in angel investors having a clear and guiding investment philosophy? Or is it best to evaluate each opportunity on its own merits?
It all depends on one's motives. If you don't start from a financial point of view, you will probably end up losing money. But even if you do start with a purely financially driven evaluation process, there are plenty of interesting companies to choose from in every sector. All young companies are risky, and it's always advisable to diversify your portfolio. If you want to make money, it's probably a good idea to think about investing in ten to twenty companies at a minimum. It's easy to fall in love with ideas, but really, execution makes the difference between success and failure. Past execution is a good predictor of future execution. That's why angels are always looking for entrepreneurs who have had a successful exit. Angel groups are super-important too. Doing enough due diligence as an individual is pretty onerous. The group can perform that role en masse, or as an individual investor.

In what ways—be it through marketing, efficient debt profile, or product/service focus— can an entrepreneur make her company or concept more appealing to an angel investor?
Angels always want a clean balance sheet going in. We want to know that the money's going towards future value creation, not paying down past value creation. Maybe that's not logical, but it's true.

Entrepreneurs really need to be out there. Stirring the water, making a splash, trying to crescendo a bunch of attention at the closing of a round. Of course, this is very hard to do! Especially without the benefit of expensive communications professionals. Thus, most entrepreneurs are on the hunt for product demonstrations and promotional ideas that create a lot of buzz for very little money.

Watch what other entrepreneurs do. Goldie Blocks was particularly brilliant this year. They capitalized on negative stereotypes about girls as engineers and provoked a lot of attention with their aggressive use of copyright-protected music in promotional videos. The controversy actually landed them a sponsored spot in the Super Bowl. That's a 10.

In your years as an angel investor, which would you count as your most memorable and your most forgettable experiences—and why?
Most memorable? Giving a young CEO high-end advice on how to handle a predatory partner. It was a life-or-death moment for the company in a conflict over rights and rates. The entrepreneur just took the advice, executed perfectly, and saved the day. He's a natural. You make lots of little saves and lots of introductions, and all of them are satisfying and memorable. In that way it's kind of like being a parent, I guess.

The forgettable? I wish! The "repetitive stress injury" is being involved with inexperienced executives who don't take coaching very well. They almost always fail. It's a really tough balancing act. Stubbornness is not confidence, but they can look similar.

Are there any parting words of advice or wisdom that you would offer to current or prospective entrepreneurs? What about prospective angel investors?

To entrepreneurs I would say, "Every day is a struggle to separate the important from the urgent from the email! It's incredibly hard to keep doing the most important work when there is such an endless amount of work."

To the angels I would say, "Read my friend David Rose's new book, *Angel Investing: The Gust Guide to Making Money and Having Fun Investing in Start-ups*. If I had this book five years ago, I might not have had more fun, but I definitely would have made more money."

Talking about Entrepreneurship

*There are many ways to float an idea, build a product, and grow a venture.
The following interviews address the numerous kinds of entrepreneurial
pursuits that designers are doing. Some succeed, while others fail.
In either case the experience is worth the struggle. Or is it?*

Todd Oldham

MASTER OF MANY MÉTIERS

It takes only a brief scan of his website to see that Oldham has had ten lifetimes of entrepreneurial activity rolled into one. He is known for his fashions, which triggered a TV series, interior design, movies, toys, products, books, and more. How to juggle the various activities and be entirely sustainable is a feat everyone with similar ambitions is anxious to learn.

When it comes to design entrepreneurship, you've covered the world, so to speak. From graphic design to publishing, from product to interior design (furniture, textiles), films, and, of course, fashion. So, why so many different ventures and adventures?

I have indeed had many working adventures in design and I am so grateful for them all, even the truly nightmarish ones, like working for Gap Inc., because there is always something to learn. For better or worse, my specifically tuned taste level and skill sets stay with me no matter what the medium, so it is very easy to shift gears and materials. I always embrace the realization I had in high school that I am basically unemployable and would be better served creating my own opportunities, a path that suits my kaleidoscopic interests.

Do you set aside specific time frames to work on any one or two of your disciplines? Or is it as the muse hits?

I do set times for specific projects, but I like working on several at the same time in shorter bursts. My work habits match my natural rhythms, which come alive at night. I love working big and fast.

And does working in one discipline influence entrepreneurship in another?

Indeed! If you are doing it right.

To me, the common denominator is design. Do you have another thread that runs through all your endeavors?

Design is important, but now the idea of being in service is a vital motivation. I do not want to be a part of any situation that is just "more." The world does not need more.

You have produced for Target and Fellissimo, among other outlets. Do you always retain your rights to your wares? Is L-7 Designs Inc. an actual corporate entity that houses all your work?

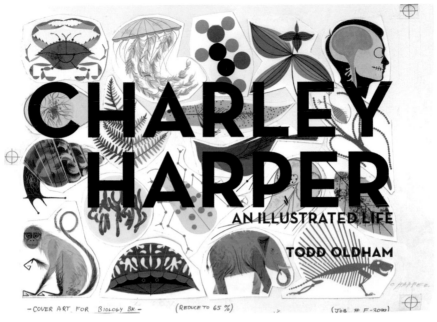

CHARLEY HARPER

AN ILLUSTRATED LIFE

TODD OLDHAM

—COVER ART FOR BIOLOGY BK—   (REDUCE TO 65 %)   (JOB # F-2090)

I do retain the rights to all of my works and trademarks. I have in the past sold parts but now own them all back again. Here is great advice. Do not sell your trademarks. The company you sold it to will change management in a short time and you will get screwed. I have had a front row seat to this situation enough times to know: never again.

8NC&FSPBJ8NC&FSPBJ
4EIZQ1WAH4EIZQ1WAH
DX9GKUY67DX9GKUY67
V5LR3MOT2ALEXANDER
8NC&FSPBJ8NCGIRARD
4EIZQ1WAH4EIZQ1WAH
DX9GKUY67DX9GKUY67
V5LR3MOT2V5LR3MOT2
8NC&FSPBJ8NC&FSPBJ
4EIZQ1WAH4EIZQ1WAH
DX TODD OLDHAM & KIERA COFFEE DX9GKUY67
V5LR3MOT2V5LR3MOT2
8NC&FSPBJ8NC&FSPBJ

Let's discuss, specifically, toys and books. They intersect, don't they?

Making anything for children requires the most dedicated effort you can summon. Toys and books can help shape young minds into national treasures, so we take our work for the young very seriously.

You don't own a publishing company, but you've done your books with one, AMMO.
How does that work? Can you do pretty much anything you want? Or are the marketing constraints in place?

I have worked with several publishers over the years, but I have done the most work with AMMO. The publisher, Steve Crist, is like my brother, and we make great stuff together. The relationship an author has with their publisher is so important to success. Mutual respect and integrity are paramount, as bookmaking is not for pussies. I most often come up with my own books, but sometimes Steve will suggest an idea, which is always great. I design and produce all of my books in-house, turning them in on hard drives. I love not getting notes, a blessing for which I count my lucky stars. I only make odd books that are hard to market, so Steve and I are up for the less-easy ride.

You've published books on Ed Emberley, Alexander Girard, and Charley Harper, as well as series of kid fashion and craft books. What determines what you'll devote yourself to?

My books seem to find me in always strange ways, so I keep my ears open for signs. I love celebrating secret masters like Charley or Mr. Girard. The books function as beacons of possibilities for folks that don't choose the normal roads. It does take a supernatural devotion to your subjects. Books are very laborious and must be perfect. There is no room in the world for bad books, especially bad art books!

How do the books influence the toys? And what is the reason behind making crayons, blocks, and other toys and games?

When we started on the book *Kid Made Modern*, it quickly became clear there was room in the world for high-quality art materials and experiences for children, so we just set out to make them. The learning, growth, and confidence that occur in making art create great humans. We believe it is that simple.

What has been your most successful product? And what is your favorite of the lot?

I have no way to gauge this question exactly as we all have different definitions of success, but to me, success is if I feel my designs have fully bloomed, not attached to sales outcomes or comments. That said, I am completely amazed that we have sold over $4 million of construction paper pads! Can you imagine?

As a business, do you work hands on, or do you focus on creative?

Both. You must be able to do everything at your job; not that you have to do all the work, but the empathy that comes from knowing makes for kind workplaces.

Todd Oldham is a brand. How did you get to be that? Was it conscious on your part?

Me as brand has always made me very uncomfortable. I just kept making stuff and people noticed and still do, but it will never stop being kind of weird.

Do you have a specific business model?

Yes, she is a size 4. We also work in pack mentality, group together, and conquer with a smile!

Peter Buchanan-Smith

MAKING THE BEST STUFF

Peter Buchanan-Smith always had an entrepreneurial bent that was underscored by artistic passions. These passions manifest in a variety of post-graduate endeavors. He published his first book, *Speck,* right out of school and cofounded an independent publishing house. Then he became art director of the *New York Times* OpEd page, design consultant for Isaac Mizrahi, creative director of *PAPER* magazine. Every time Buchanan-Smith got too comfortable, he started something new. He founded Best Made Company in 2009 because he saw a need for a better axe: "an evocative tool that played an indispensable role in his life working on cattle farms and paddling and portaging the lakes of Northern Canada," he says. Today that company has expanded to sell a variety of outdoor accessories and fashions and is primed to be the next big thing.

How did you become a design entrepreneur?

There were many catalysts, but the driving force was just a love/need to make things. Since my first book, *Speck* (my thesis for the MFA design program at SVA), I've always been fascinated with the role objects play in our lives. With Best Made, I set out to create the stage where my own objects can play off one another. And now I'm busy crafting that story, keeping the actors in motion, the audience entertained.

What triggered your interest in well-made axes?

You can either hate an axe or love it, but I'll be damned if you can deny how useful it is at starting a fire! Around 2009 I was going through a divorce and an overwhelming series of calamitous events, and I thought: "If all I had was completely and utterly lost, what's the one thing I'd need most?" And the more I came to reckon with the axe, the more it made sense as a real part of me: my tool and perch for many greater things.

How did you bridge from this axe fixation into becoming Best Made, a veritable urban J. Peterman?

I bridged the fixation by not fixating, and keeping the mission bigger than myself. I set out to get people to the campfire, and for that I knew they'd need a well-made axe. And once they had the axe, maybe they'd need the first aid kit, the warm wool blanket, or the right waxed jacket.

What has the process of making a business entailed?

Setting realistic expectations while constantly striving to improve the reality we're in.

You currently have a store and have produced a print catalog. What is your business structure?

The best virtues of small business—and the envy of all big business—are freedom and agility. As a designer, I am fortunate in that I'm trained to make things materialize, often under tight deadlines. I take all of the product photography, I write the copy, I design the website and the catalog, and that makes my job thrilling, and it gives the company soul.

You've certainly grown. But do you foresee more growth?

We're just getting started. Between clothing, home goods, edible products, camp gear, books, and accessories, we've spanned so many categories in just five years. All that hard work has taught us, and we're becoming more masters of these domains. Now we're perfectly poised to start drilling down, and to continue to expand upon our mission and reach more people.

Have you had to hire various specialists?

We've hired photographers, filmmakers, lawyers, clothing designers, bag designers, type designers, and graphic designers, and I hope many other characters as we grow. Having a clear and consistent mission is critical to working with so many people. Everyone's gotta be on the same page, from the top down.

Do you push your comfort zone, or are you in a comfortable place?

As we grow, I seem to have little choice in the matter—my comfort zone is automatically challenged, all the time. As we grow, every quarter seems like I'm running a new company. New staff,

new product, new customers: they all change the dynamic. They can throw dirt on me when I get too comfortable!

You began as a graphic designer. What element of graphic design do you maintain in the Best Made scheme?

There's the literal day-to-day graphic design that I am still connected to, and then there's the art of designing a company/brand. Now that I am CEO of Best Made, I am less career focused and more company driven. I bring my skills and the mind-set of a designer to bear as I shape and grow the company. We're now seeing just how good it is for a company to have a designer—or one with a design mind-set—as its founder/leader. (Just ask Apple!)

Can you describe how you are branding BEST MADE?

The Best Made X is above all a mark of authority, but it should impart some sense of humanity, and even playfulness. I want Best Made to be that place most of us only knew as kids, when possibilities were endless, and expertise was for the grown-ups!

Is there a goal at this point, or are you only thinking about the here and now?

The goal is to keep the momentum driving forward, our intentions good and grounded, and then the fun and excitement will follow. We're just about to turn five years old, and that's a major milestone. I try not to think too far out, or look too far back.

Maira Kalman

HER PASSION COMETH

Maira Kalman, an illustrator, author, and designer, has created many covers for the *New Yorker*, including the famous map of "New Yorkistan" (created with Rick Meyerowitz). Her over two dozen children's books include *Max Makes a Million*, *Stay Up Late*, *Swami on Rye*, and *What Pete Ate*. She also has designed fabric for Isaac Mizrahi, accessories for Kate Spade, sets for the Mark Morris Dance Company, and, recently, two books celebrating the collections of the Cooper Hewitt. In addition to her entrepreneurial passions, her paintings and drawings are shown at the Julie Saul Gallery in Manhattan.

How do you define yourself?

In my sunnier moments I think of myself as an artist/writer/journalist. Wandering around. Going back to my studio. Telling a story that is both sad and funny.

Do you ever think of yourself as a brand?

Not as a brand, but as a person who is curious about many things.

Your entrepreneurship started with products by M&Co. What are your products now?

That is a good question. Mostly my products are books that I write and/or illustrate. Or I create work as an artist-at-large for magazines. So narrative content is my product. Along the way, products have been made by other companies: A shower curtain of NEWYORKISTAN (The *New Yorker* cover done in collaboration with Rick Meyerowitz), a puzzle from *Fireboat: The Heroic Adventures of the John J. Harvey*. I have created designs for Kate Spade, and that was fun. I am working on a few watch ideas. And a lamp that I would like to make in collaboration with Rick Meyerowitz. But those are taking forever because basically I am not interested in creating products. There is a lot of other work to do.

How do you determine what will be an editorial, gallery, or product idea? What is your mechanism for making something entrepreneurial?

I used to be more determined about making products. As I said, I am not so inclined anymore. Books are a passion for me. And, I think, always will be. I am fortunate to have a gallery that will sell the paintings from my books and articles. That is a wonderful double life for a painting.

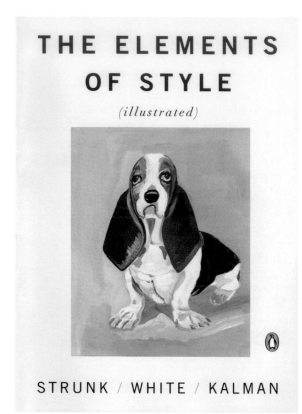

You've had many children's and adult books. Are these routinely published by others or have you retained ownership?

I have never self-published. That seems like a tremendous and boring pain in the neck. I am lucky that there are publishers who want to take on the books. The publisher has the rights to publish and distribute for some amount of years, whatever that is. But I own the original art and can do what I please with those.

Are there any limitations to what you take on as an artist or producer?

The only criteria, at this point, is if it is interesting. I won't add fun, because that is an elusive notion. But there has to be some amount of fun and intellectual satisfaction for me.

I don't really illustrate other people's articles anymore. I want to create the text and art. I am not apathetic or oblivious about fees. Some projects are sensational, but don't pay so well. Usually there is a mix of better paying and not so great. A common situation. So you have an equation: time/money/interest plus instinct minus rent you have to pay = decision about job.

Dallas Graham

HEALING BIRDS

In December of 2012, Dallas Graham's younger sister phoned him from Seattle to say she just had learned that a mutual friend from childhood had a son, Mitchell, with Duchenne muscular dystrophy. The ten-year-old boy was dying. Their immediate and joint response was, "What can we possibly do for them? For him?" As Graham thought about the "certain uncertainties," what he describes as a "star-thought" landed on him. It felt distinctly like an avian character he created, "Red Fred lighting on my shoulder and whispering in my ear: 'We want to make a book with him.'" He emailed the family, begging forgiveness for "encroaching on anything that would seem strange or unethical and at the same time," he told them, "children love my birds and my birds love children." They graciously accepted the invitation to make a book for their son. Three months later, Graham received a message that Mitchell was in the final few days and that the family was coming together to be with him. Days later, thousands witnessed his passing. The grieving family had kept friends and relatives updated through social media. "Thousands grieved and mourned," said Graham "So did my birds." Birds? Enter The Red Fred Project and The Jolly Troop. I asked Graham to explain the genesis of his social entrepreneurship and his Jolly Troop of diacritical birds.

How did you become involved with the Red Fred Project?

That day [of Mitchell's passing] I determined exactly what I wanted to do. I wanted to create joy and legacies. I wanted to create original, one-of-a-kind stories with children with critical illnesses, self-publish their book, and then put it into their hands and say, "Way to go! You did it. You made a book!" Additionally, the proceeds of each printed book would go to the child's/family's medical expenses. This is what the Red Fred Project is.

Is there a particular issue in your own family that you wanted to address?

Not particularly. But I do understand, to a certain extent, what death and departure of a little one does to a person. When I was nine years old, my cousin (whom I was very close to) died from the effects of leukemia. His death had a profound influence on me at a young age. I definitely see threads of that experience in my intention now.

Was Mitchell your first subject?

Truthfully, there were two "firsts." Mitchell Jones was the boy I talked about earlier. He died before we were able to work on his book. The second "first" is Nathan Glad. I was introduced to him through a man named Stephen Stauffer. Stephen runs an organization that improves the lives of children with very rare diseases. It's called Angel's Hands. When I called him and explained what the Red Fred Project was and that I was seeking a child to work with, he said, "I know exactly who you need to meet." That's how I met Nathan.

This has to be an emotionally wrenching project. Has it consumed your professional practice?

Yes and no. The first thought is that working with children with critical illnesses can potentially be very weighty, especially if the child's life won't last much longer. Additionally, I am not around this special demographic in my professional or personal life much—unlike doctors, nurses, home-care providers, therapists. However, I find that by engaging them with their imaginations and story-making ideas, there is a lot of stardust material that shapes the time and environment when we work together. How do I say this without sounding insensitive: there isn't a lot of "pity" in this project; conversely, there is an abundance of creativity and life and fantastic conjuring, which colors the incredible life this child is living. These are magical, creative children who have faced significant challenges in short lifetimes with humor, compassion, and wisdom-filled stories to share. The Red Fred Project gives those children and their stories a voice.

Are you a designer?

I suppose I am . . . and I'm not trying to be obtuse, either. I create with images, typography, photography, and writing in all manner of creative ways. That's what I've done for years. Does that mean I'm a designer? You tell me.

What is the status of the project now?

We completed our first book with our first creative! Nathan's book is called *Climbing with Tigers*. We celebrated the accomplishment by having a book signing downtown. Hundreds came to support and meet him. It was completely captivating to witness firsthand. We are in discussion with a family in Idaho who has a six-year-old daughter with stage-three melanoma, and there is a teenager in California with a rare brain cancer who has expressed interest, too. People are writing in, asking if they can help find the children. It's a fascinating and humbling thing to watch.

What is the future of the project?

The Red Fred Project's goal is to create 50 books with 50 children across the 50 states. Once that is completed, we hope to share this same creative process with thousands of children. I believe we can do that by inviting creatives in every city to get involved, if they'd like to. My hope is that they will take the initiative and reach out to us. We'll send them the assets they'll need to keep the books within the style of the Red Fred Project, but otherwise I want to encourage them to walk out of their studio, take a train ride or bus ride or car ride to a home with a child with a critical illness. I want them to have their own experience creating a hard-bound legacy of joy and creativity, topped with a star.

Adrian Shaughnessy, Unit Editions

NEW MODEL FOR BOOKMAKING

Prior to founding the London-based independent design book publisher Unit Editions, the partners, Adrian Shaughnessy and Tony Brook, both ran design studios. Before meeting, Brook had done some self-publishing, while Shaughnessy had plenty of experience working with traditional publishers. Adrian had found it frustrating to accomplish what he wanted, so their meeting was timely. As design book addicts, they both had the itch to see certain books in print, and realized that if this was not going to happen through traditional means, they would have to do it themselves. Unit Editions has published some important books in just a few years and developed into a sustainable business. Here are some insights into a few of their books.

Starting a partnership is difficult enough. Starting a publishing venture these days may be foolhardy. What was your plan from the outset?

It requires a certain lunacy. A deranged love of books helps. Fortunately we have a levelheaded business partner in Trish Finegan. Trish stops us going bust and keeps a firm grip on finances, production, and resources.

Your books started modestly. Did you invest your own funds?

Unit Editions is entirely self-funded. Our first title went through the book trade, and the experience nearly scuppered [sank] us. But it also taught us a lesson: if we were going to be independent, then we really had to be totally independent. This meant no book trade, no distributors, and most importantly, no Amazon. So we sell nearly all our books from our website. I was talking to a mainstream publisher the other day and he said, "You are a super-niche publisher." And I suppose we are.

It did not take long for your projects to develop into what I call "adult" books. Ambitious in scope and size. How were you able to make these leaps?

"Adult" books? I don't remember publishing any porn or erotica! But I think I know what you mean. Early successes with our books on Total Design and Supergraphics gave us the confidence to become more ambitious. Our book on Herb

Lubalin was the first of a run of three major monographs; the other two were Ken Garland and, more recently, FHK Henrion. All of these books require huge amounts of work. We photograph nearly all the visual material we include in our books. This means long hours in dusty archives. Tony leads the design team, creating covers and layouts. I work on texts and general editorial duties. It's a lot of work and has to be fitted in around all our other tasks. But it's strange: no matter how busy you are, there's always time for the things you love.

Your books do not sell in retail stores. Why not?

We actually supply a number of bookshops—but only ones we have a personal relationship with. Using our web-only model means we get paid before we ship a title. With the book trade you have to wait months for payment from distributors. To function in the book trade, we would have needed to raise funds through investors, or take out bank loans. Doing it this way we are self-funding. Each book pays for the next one. I sometimes regret that our books are not in more bookshops. Not just for the sales, but for the fact that books in bookshops enter the cultural ecosystem in a way that is different from the Internet; people can handle them, be surprised by them, feel the heft!

There's one other thing worth mentioning. Because our main focus is not on retail sales, we can take liberties with our covers. They don't have to have titles on the front.

Your strategy is to pre-sell through the web. Has this proven successful?

The pre-order sell is really important to us. We offer a healthy discount for pre-ordering, and we do free shipping to anywhere in the world. People in South America and New Zealand tell us it's something they really value. They are put off buying books from Europe because of high shipping charges.

Restaurant managers always have to predict how much food they'll need to stock. How do you predict how many "units" you'll need to produce?

The Unit Editions Gourmet Restaurant? There's an idea. We have a strict no-big-print-runs policy. We are really disciplined about that. Huge overstocks are the path to ruin. Small, high-quality print runs only! All our early titles have sold out, so we are not sitting on piles of unsold books racking up huge storage charges.

How do you create demand for your "products"?

By making the books as freaking good as possible. All our books are highly de-signed artifacts (but never at the expense of the content) and come with high pro-duction values. Second, we always find out what it is that makes a historical figure, or contemporary subject, interesting or relevant to a contemporary audience and present this through clear texts, essays, interviews, and good captions. Get that right, and the demand creates itself.

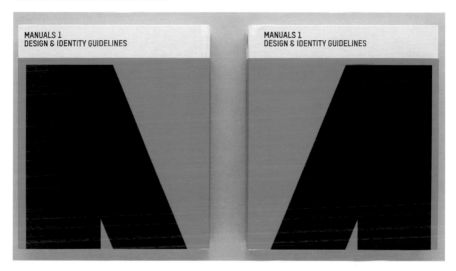

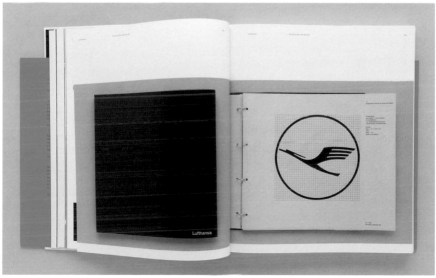

Are your books considered "limited editions"?

There are always a few thousand copies of each title. I don't think this qualifies for "limited edition" status.

You clearly fill a need. Do you foresee testing those boundaries with even more ambitious projects?

We thought our most recent title—*Manuals 1*—was a high-risk title. Both Tony and I love these big slabs of ring-bound delight, and we knew there was a small and dedicated audience for a book on this subject, but we have been amazed by the response. It is our second-best-selling title after *Herb Lubalin*. But yes, we want to be more ambitious and expand our repertoire. There are a few titles in the pipeline that might surprise people.

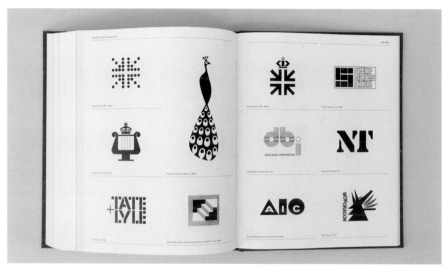

How long was the Henrion book in the making?

Tony started talking to Marion Wesel-Henrion (FHK Henrion's widow) a few years ago. There had been attempts by others to get a Henrion monograph off the ground—but they had all failed. With Marion's support, our book eventually became a reality. It took about fourteen months of solid work to complete. The project began with the photographing of Henrion's work (many hundreds of specimens) held in the University of Brighton Design Archives. This was followed by about nine months of writing, a lengthy and intense design period, followed by printing. Lots of weekends got swallowed up along the way.

Given that you are an independent publisher, what is the investment in a volume of this kind?

In terms of time, the investment is incalculable. We couldn't begin to amortize our time. But in all other areas we are cautious, lean, and self-contained. Apart from printing, proofreading, and indexing, we are nearly self-sufficient, so our financial outlay is as low as it can get.

Did you have an idea of how his work, which is not as well-known as it might be in the United States, would do in your marketplace?

We were nervous, frankly. Even people with a strong interest in twentieth-century graphic design sometimes look blank when Henrion's name is mentioned. But we trusted that as soon as people saw the work, they would recognize him as a bona fide design genius—which he undoubtedly was. And that's pretty much what has happened. The book is selling well all over the world, and I've given a few talks to students in the UK and Europe, and they get him instantly. Our faith has been rewarded.

What is the extent of your marketplace?

Because we sell 95 percent of our books via our website (no Amazon, and only a few friendly bookshops whom we deal with directly), we are shipping to all quarters of the globe. The world is our marketplace. Recently we've had orders for the Henrion book from Peru, Vietnam, Romania, and even . . . wait for it . . . the USA!

What is the break-even point?

It varies. We print only small quantities of our books (usually 2,000 or 3,000). The break-even point is when we sell enough books to finance the next one. We have six books planned for 2014.

What did you learn about Henrion that you did not know?

I learned that he is the most important British (though German-born) graphic designer ever. No one in the UK comes close to matching his intellectual heft or his range of activities. He left Germany, age nineteen, to escape the Nazis and trained in Paris as a poster artist. He came to Britain in the 1930s and worked for the allied war effort—the British, the Dutch, and Americans. (He has some very flattering things to say about working for the US military and their largesse in comparison to the poor, penny-pinching Brits. For example, he cycled to the British HQ in the morning, but in the afternoon he was picked up in a staff car by the US military, where he oversaw

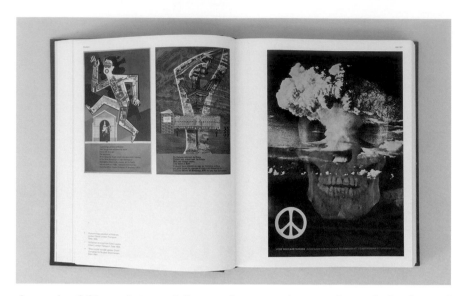

the work of fifteen designers.) During the war and in its aftermath, he designed posters in a style that we now we see as dated, but even here he was a progressive, and made use of photography at a time when everyone else was using crayons and airbrushes.

In the 1950s he reinvented himself and became one of the pioneers of corporate identity (his school friend was Walter Landor). Henrion was amongst the first in Europe, and certainly in the UK, to offer a systematic and ultrarational approach to identity. Many of his best identities are still in use forty to fifty years after he created them: KLM is perhaps the most famous.

He did more than anyone to professionalize the British design industry. He took it from a cottage industry (crayons and airbrushes!) to a fully professionalized industry. But in the 1980s, when design firms were launching themselves on the stock market, driving Porsches, and opening offices around the world, Henrion recoiled from this reversal of priorities. For him, it had to be about the work, not the money. He spent his last decade teaching, writing, and evangelizing on behalf of design. At a time when it wasn't fashionable to say it, he maintained that a designer had a duty to society that went beyond helping to sell stuff. One of his most celebrated works is a poster that he did (unpaid, of course) for the Campaign for Nuclear Disarmament (CND).

What did you learn about publishing that you did not know?

Well, it's counterintuitive, but our expensive books sell better than our cheap ones. As e-books and tablets grow in popularity, and at a time when you can see nearly everything online, we've discovered that people (in our case, designers) seem to value printed books more than ever. But it has to be books that push all known boundaries, and text, design, and printing have to be best in show.

John Taylor and Dianne Dubler

KUBABA BESPOKE BOOKS

Almost immediately after meeting in 1970, John and Dianne set off for Afghanistan, Nepal, and India. After eight years of traveling—and running three small, art-related businesses—they wanted to return home and develop a career that allowed them to work with both photography and art. Gillett Griffin, then curator of Pre-Columbian Art at Princeton University, suggested they combine their two passions. He pointed out that the quality of most photography of works-of-art was terrible, and John remarked that what photographers were being paid to do it was pretty bad as well. So the plan was to provide photography to the art world at a much higher level of quality and charge prices more in line with commercial work. Over the next thirty-five years, they photographed architecture and gardens, works of art, jewelry, and objects for most of the major art book publishers, many of the world's museums, and numerous private clients. They produced images

for over 250 art books, for a client list that has included—among many others—Madeleine Albright, Elizabeth Taylor, Yoko Ono, Lord Jacob Rothschild, and The White House.

While working in England on *Waddesdon, The Biography of a Rothschild House* for Harry Abrams, they were introduced to Ferdinand Rothschild's Red Book. Privately produced in the 1890s by the creator of Waddesdon, this leather-bound edition was made exclusively for his family and friends. The Red Book told the story of Waddesdon's development and was illustrated with photographs of the house and its construction as well as its formidable collections. It was the ultimate "take-away." A few years later, as a gift for her husband, a client asked them to produce a "red book" about their Hudson Valley estate. Kubaba Bespoke Books was born from that idea.

You began as photographers. Did you feel that your work was not getting the best editorial care?

We always got great care, but we also loved developing our own projects.

How did you transition from freelance photographers to book packagers?

From the beginning we were occasionally asked to produce private publications for galleries and artists. Our shared love of books and their design and typography made this a natural and welcome diversion from our day-to-day photography work. After producing the images for the book on Waddesdon Manor and our exposure to the original owner's Red Book, it seemed a good idea to find book projects for private individuals with interesting and important homes and collections where we controlled the imagery, design, text, and book production. The focus of our photography work had always been on architecture, interiors, works of art, antiquities, and jewelry, so books like this are a natural for us.

Originally, most of your work was as photographers only, then you began to package "art" books. How did this come about and why the break with traditional publishing methods?

We saw a market that tied together our photographic skills, experience, and interests in the "book arts" at a time when publishing to the trade was having a hard time.

Then it wasn't the best time to jump into publishing—or was it?

Producing private publications removed us from the vagaries of the market. Those books are well funded and most are not for sale. Though paid well for our work, we seldom made money after our books to the trade were published. So there was no loss of a residual income as we moved into bespoke publishing.

Unlike most packagers, you tell the stories through images and text. How do you decide what project to devote yourself to?

The project must be interesting to us, and we need to have the time available. However, over many years and many projects, we have learned that an immersion into almost any subject, often something we are not familiar with, results in developing a surprising interest in and affection for that subject and usually for the clients themselves. We consider it a privilege to work with such extraordinary material and people.

As an example, we are about to start work on a private collection of petrified wood made over forty years by the man who dug the trees out of the ground. The sixty-six examples in the collection are the finest pieces of the thousands he collected. We knew nothing about the subject before meeting the collector, but the book we will produce will be an extraordinary representation not only of the collection but also of the formidable efforts of the collector to put it together.

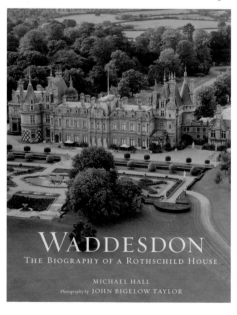

Do you work with others? Or is it just you two?

For our photography we use assistants and we hire helicopter pilots, book design-ers, writers, printers, and binders. Otherwise, it's just us overseeing everything.

What has been your business model that allows you to make the books you want to do? The care you put into each project: Is it indeed profitable?

So far. We price our work high enough that we can concentrate on at least three or four projects a year. While we base the photography portion of a book on day rates, we also add a percentage of the costs of the other elements, as well as a fee for handling the entire project.

You've entered into the universe of "bespoke" books. In a way, that's how Harry Abrams started. Would you call these vanity books?

One could call them that, though we do not. We see them as works of art in their own right, celebrating the creation of extraordinary architecture, landscapes, and im-portant collections—much of which will probably be dispersed as time moves on. The books are "portraits of accomplishment" that will exist long after our clients are gone and the homes and collections are no longer intact.

Even if a publisher wanted to publicly promote these books, most of our clients, for many reasons, are not interested. Since privacy is essential to these people, and they are only distributing to a select few, the discretion and high quality we provide is their best way to realize such a book.

How do you find the subjects for the bespoke books? Does the investment derive from the subjects?

Our entire career has mostly run on word of mouth. Our projects today come from—or are referred by—people we know or have worked with in the past, from people who have seen our work and contact us through our website (www.kubaba.com) and, of course, from constant networking. The client pays for everything.

Obviously, the big question: Are books sustainable? How do you keep them viable?

We keep them viable by maintaining a viable need for them. Our work focuses on the production of limited-edition, privately commissioned books that document—with a vibrant eclecticism—important homes and collections for their owners and for posterity. Books are among the most meaningful artifacts of society. They will never go out of fashion.

Do you foresee branching into the digital realm, or is your philosophy based on the essence of fine bookmaking?

We make books. We make beautiful books! No one knows how digital information will be accessed in the future and what will be compatible with today's technology. Books, however, have been proven to withstand the centuries. Some have lasted five hundred years and more and have always been valued as works of art and prized possessions. It is difficult to see how digital technology will replace a large-format, illustrated book with something more satisfying. That being said, everything that goes into a book today is digital.

What is your biggest challenge?

Successfully interpreting for our clients, in book form, the result of a significant portion of their life's fortune and creativity. Making sure that the book is worthy. To achieve this, the relationship with our clients has to be one of mutual respect. There develops an intimacy that is essential for these books to really sing. Though each project is different, with every one we have done so far, there has been significant client input. On the whole, this has resulted in productive collaborations and beautiful books.

What are your greatest joys as publishers?

The people we meet and visiting the worlds into which they invite us. And then to hand them a finished book on what they have created. That is a real joy!

Daniel Stark

BARKING UP THE PAPER TREE

Daniel Stark of Stark Design/Agency Orange says that paper has played a significant part in his personal and professional life. Of course, designers are conditioned to be paper aficionados, but so are children and adults of all ages. PaperMade is Stark's attempt at pushing paper to the limits of usability as medium for a plethora of games and hobbies. Although he sold his idea to a larger publisher, the idea for this venture rests firmly on his shoulders.

Is this toy book, Paper Pups *by PaperMade, your first book?*
No, this is my second book. The first, *Stoked: The Evolution of Action Sports*, was done with a partner and released in 2006.

What prompted your interest?
I've always been fascinated with paper and want to push paper to its limit. I try this whenever I can in work we do for clients, so PaperMade is really an extension of that. I first had the idea in 2004 and developed games—chess, checkers, tic-tac-toe—out of paper. When I finally got a publisher, we had developed a bunch of ideas and decided that *Paper Pups* would be the best place to start and that consumers would love them.

How involved were you in the production?
Completely. While the publisher, powerHouse, chose the printer and is responsible for the manufacturing, we chose papers and did as much as we could to control quality and mitigate problems.

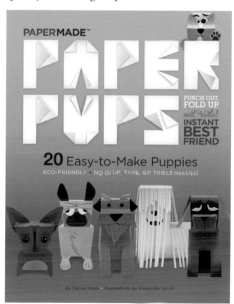

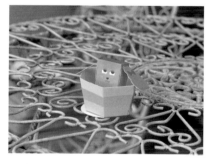

How involved are you in the distribution and promotion of the project?

I'm not involved in the distribution—that is Random House's role. But I have used my contacts and friends to supplement the promotional outreach that the publisher is doing already.

What is your goal in business terms?

My dream is to sell fifty thousand copies or more! I know that may be a crazy idea, but to be honest, the book has already exceeded my initial goals in that we pre-sold over seven thousand copies, and the initial response seems to be overwhelmingly positive.

What has been your primary means of getting the word out?

I'm using every media I know to get the word out and have been posting "teasers" of images on Facebook for the last couple of weeks. As we get closer to the on-sale date, we will continue the buildout of the website with videos and more info on the

book, populate a YouTube channel, set up a Twitter account and maybe a Facebook page as well as Instagram. We're really hoping that design and consumer blogs like Paper Pups and help us spread the word.

Is publishing this an act of love or passion?

Ha ha, this is probably both—mixed with some insanity! I have been pushing to get this book published for over seven years, so if nothing else it's an act of determination and, yes, love. We've got at least a hundred more ideas for more books and are working on three more for next year. If this one does well, we will be filled with passion to meet our existing love for the concept.

What are your future entrepreneurial plans?

We have a dozen more ideas for PaperMade the brand, and personally, I have one invention, already patented, that I am working to get to market and three other consumer products in the pipeline. On another front, I have a new start-up company with partners based in Bangkok, Thailand, and two more businesses I'm really hoping to get off the ground: one is a travel-based business and the other is a digital social game called Realitree (which you can read about at therealitree.org).

Heather Burkman

THE GO-COMB EXPERIENCE

Brooklyn-based Heather Burkman's background is in fashion and business. She studied design, marketing, and entrepreneurship at Cornell University, and after a year and a half working in fashion merchandising, she moved over to marketing and worked at Etsy for four years. She says it was interesting making the switch from helping build a platform for independent artists and designers to being one herself.

How long have you been doing entrepreneurial ventures?

I've always had an entrepreneurial streak. My first "business" was designing and making custom prom dresses in my hometown while I was in high school. In college I took several entrepreneurship classes, and even won a business plan competition, for a conceptual product design company catering to the elderly. I ran several Etsy shops and have always toyed with the idea of running my own business, and in May 2013 I officially quit my day job to run go-comb full-time.

How did the designed go-comb venture begin?

I was inspired by my uncle, who after dinner one night pulled out his wallet, and there was the ubiquitous black plastic comb awkwardly sticking out the side. I thought, "why doesn't someone just design a comb that fits in the wallet?" I learned how to laser cut, began prototyping, and opened an Etsy shop a few weeks later. I've gone through many iterations, materials, and production processes since then.

Was this built on a business plan?

Not officially. I built the business with a few goals in mind: Make it profitable. From the beginning I wanted to pursue this business (and quit a job I liked) only if it was going to make money. I started out with on-demand manufacturing (laser cutting) so that I didn't need to invest in expensive tooling or holding large amounts of inventory. I knew the margins required to be successful in both retail and wholesale, and factored this in to my decisions. As I built up profits and learned more about my target market as well as the strengths and weaknesses of my product, I began to reinvest in the business as it grew. I didn't leave my job until I was earning a modest "salary" from go-comb and felt fairly confident about future growth.

Make it scalable. Having sold various handmade products in the past (clothing, scarves), I knew that if I wanted to make a living from this, I would need to find a way to outsource the production, so that I could focus primarily on growing the business. I started with laser cutting but have since moved to other processes which can scale significantly, from the actual comb manufacturing to packaging and, soon, shipping.

Make it work with my lifestyle. My husband and I are avid travelers, and we soon see ourselves starting a family. I want to build a business that contributes to our income, but doesn't run my life. I'm outsourcing as much as possible, so that I don't need to employ lots of people and operate a large office. Manufacturing and packaging already happen elsewhere. Recently I hired a PR firm, and in the future I hope to also hire out shipping fulfillment and accounting. My goal this year is to hire someone who can be my right hand, and ideally that would be enough for a while.

How do you manufacture?

The combs are chemically etched and coated in a smooth finish. The production starts in China and is finished in the United States, including packaging.

Are you the only one who designs?

I'm the only designer for go-comb, but I've also begun to collaborate with other designers who are skilled in areas I'm not. Julia Rothman was my most recent collaborator, and she designed a whimsical print for our plastic version. It's been very popular and I'm excited to continue working with other designers in the future.

Are the combs the sole product?

Yes. There are various styles, from fine tooth (great for short hair and beards) to regular to mirror. The potential reach for go-comb is so wide, and the need for brushing hair isn't in risk of going "out of trend," so I'm happy to continue growing our reach and staying relevant with fashionable designs.

How have you made the product sustainable?

The primary material is stainless steel, which is recyclable. I've also continued improving the materials so that they're as durable as possible—ideally a person's go-comb sits in their wallet, making it hard to lose, and I try to make it unbreakable. They shouldn't need to replace it every season or so, like one does with clothing or accessories. I'm also developing a new plastic version, which I want to be recyclable.

What outlets do you use to sell go-combs?

For sales we sell on our website, go-comb.com, on Amazon, and a little on Etsy. Go-combs are carried in over 170 retail shops across the United States and abroad, which you can see here: go-comb.com/stockists. We grow our wholesale business primarily through trade shows, focusing on gifts, beauty, and fashion.

We're on social media with Facebook, Instagram, and Twitter.

Can you define your audience, and how did you reach them?

Our audience is, thankfully but challengingly, huge. We sell to every gender, age, and aesthetic preference, given our variety of styles. If someone has hair or facial hair that they comb or brush, they are our audience. Most of our reach has occurred through press; we've been featured in numerous popular magazines and blogs including *Real Simple*, *New York* magazine, *Uncrate*, *Essence*, *People Style Watch*, *Cool Hunting*, *Good Housekeeping*, *Seventeen*, and more. I can confidently say we sell about 50 percent to men and 50 percent to women, and people love buying go-combs as gifts, but we really run the gamut in terms of target demographic.

How often do you change your line?

I formally introduce new styles and colors twice a year, for spring/summer and for fall/winter. My styles are influenced by fashion trends, and I personally find inspiration from textile and decorative patterns. I test new styles and finishes throughout the year as well, at a smaller scale.

What does the future have in store for this and other products?

Go-comb has a lot farther to go before I'd consider it "established." I'm working on expanding into plastic and possibly other materials so that go-combs can be offered in a greater range of price points. My goal this year is scaling sales—reaching more customers through bigger retailers and through our own sales channels. I see go-comb as a staple product, ideally establishing a stable business on its own. I hope to carve out more time for my own creative exploration in the coming year, possibly something artsy or crafty to get back to my roots.

Joey Cofone, Baron Fig

MAKING DIARIES

Joey Cofone is a graphic designer who, while still in school, entered the physical world of designing lines of sketchbooks and stationery. It's a crowded space, which he says does not bother him at all. He has carved out a niche for his Baron Fig products, but the speed that consumables are trending has forced him to stay on his toes to keep his market

What made you delve into the analog notebook field, especially with so many competitors?

Why did Facebook jump into territory that was dominated by MySpace? Why did Apple keep plugging away when the personal computer market was effectively monopolized by Microsoft's Windows? In retrospect it's easy to praise their persistence, but if they'd failed, we'd be lambasting their naïveté. I'm not saying we're Facebook or Apple, but I won't deny that they're companies we strive to learn from, whose leaders we admire. Nor am I unique in doing so.

A few years back I noticed something interesting during my time at the School of Visual Arts in NYC. I was in the graphic design program, and I used two primary tools to create work: a computer and a notebook. Same goes for my peers, but there was something peculiar going on. It seemed that while everyone was using the same computer—a Mac—there was an incredibly diverse set of notebooks being used. On top of the differing notebooks, students (myself included) were also switching books each time they had to get a new one. So on one hand we had this ubiquitous tool that everyone used, and on the other we had a tool that had zero loyalty and continuity. Looking at the analog notebook field, sure, there are a lot of players. What some see as a negative, I see as a positive. The very fact that there are a lot of players tells us something important: there's enough interest in the category to sustain different perspectives on what a notebook can be.

We navigate these waters with a simple strategy: focus on ourselves, not on our competition. Our primary goal is to continue with our unified voice: to speak to makers and the joys of ideation. We aim to make products that support this philosophy. What the other guys are doing doesn't matter much as long as we're not ignorant of it. In the end, we're looking to carve out a piece of the market that we can call our own.

How have you been able to fund this? And is your funding model sustainable?

It's easy to have an idea, hard to validate it, and even harder to sustain it. We were lucky to have Kickstarter as an option, which was unavailable just a few short years ago, to help us quickly validate our idea without putting too much capital on the table. Once the idea was validated, we had a full launch via our website. Creating

a successful Kickstarter campaign is a matter of incredible preparation. Over the course of five months, we designed a product, created sharable media, composed the Kickstarter page and video, and began spreading the word. We started the Kickstarter campaign in September 2013. Our original funding goal was $15K, and at the end of the thirty-day insanity that is a successful Kickstarter, we had surpassed our goal by eleven times raising over $168K. All in all, we presold 8,760 books to 4,242 people from forty-eight countries. The whole thing was a whirlwind adventure. As much work as we had put together in the five months preceding, those thirty days felt like the same amount crammed into a shorter time frame. I was answering nonstop emails, tweets, Facebook posts, and Instagram comments. In between reactionary efforts I was proactively contacting journalists, bloggers, designers, and anyone else that I believed matched our target market. On more than one occasion I literally landed face first in bed, sprawled out and with my shoes still on, and slept like a rock. It was exhausting, but worth it. Having a concrete end date and a light at the end of the tunnel helped.

The following March we launched our website (baronfig.com) with full web store. At the time we still had just one product, the Confidant hardcover notebook. Since then (eight months at the time of writing this) we've launched a second product, the Apprentice pocket notebook, and have sold over twenty thousand books.

You say that your format is based on the opinions of various artists and designers. How does this work?

We always begin exploring ideas by talking about our own observations and preferences. In the case of notebooks, they are tools that every one of us has been using since childhood, and whether or not we're aware of it, we all have strong preferences. Then we look to others for feedback, which in turn allows us to again internally explore new ideas. We rinse and repeat until we come up with something we love. In the case of the Confidant, we emailed over five hundred thinkers around the world—

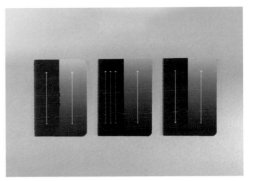

architects, designers, illustrators, writers, etc.—and asked them one simple question: "What do you like in a sketchbook or notebook?" Over 80 percent responded—which utterly blew us away—and many with extremely detailed feedback. We used their collective guidance to shape the design.

We take pride in being highly connected to our community. Feedback was integral in designing our project, launching our Kickstarter, and ultimately our company, and it continues to be at the core of our daily endeavors. Every single day, our users share their thoughts by email, twitter, Facebook, or in person. The title of our feedback page reads, "Let's make great things—together." We believe in this to the fullest.

You sell your product only online. How do you make people aware of your offerings?

Baron Fig is currently 100 percent owned and operated by myself and my partner, Adam Kornfield. We don't have tens of thousands of investor dollars to play with (by choice). This means we need to make every dollar go as absolutely far as possible. We could take $10K and buy a bunch of ads, or we could use that cash to create something that people will want to click and share without being cajoled. We achieve this goal through Baron Fig Projects, which are creative endeavors that can be consumed via the web in bite-sized portions. They run the gamut from image-based collections to exploratory videos, interactive microsites to in-person installations, and so on. With each we aim to entertain, educate, and exhibit some sort of creative collaboration.

A good example of this is the Poster Project from summer 2014. We art-directed twelve inspiring posters by thinkers from around the world, with all proceeds going to the visual and silkscreen artists. Each poster was a limited edition run of fifty, revealed one per day over the course of two weeks leading up to the sale. It was a fantastic success.

Baron Fig Projects have been covered by media such as Fast Company, Bloomberg, and Quartz, to name a few. These projects are a lot riskier than simply buying ads, but the reward is much greater. If done right, we end up making something we can be proud of, creating content that helps define our company, and putting things into the world that bring joy. It's a win-win-win.

You say that this notebook project is just the beginning of a large "culture." Can you explain what you mean?

It is not the beginning of a culture. The culture already exists, that of makers who love creating with heart. I know this because I'm one of them, and Baron Fig was created out of the passion I have for this mind-set. I remember in first grade the day I unintentionally smashed the usual inside-the-box thinking. It was first grade, and we were given an illustration to color and cut out for the bulletin board. Everyone got the same cartoon worm with big eyes and gangly limbs. We all wanted to be able to say, "Look at mine!" and have it be different from everyone else (dare I say better?). Up until this point I was playing the same game as everyone else, competing with my classmates by trying to color as uniquely as possible. After cutting out Mr. Worm I realized that I now had a bunch of scrap paper left over. Instead of throwing it away, I drew my own little accessories for him—a microphone, boombox, and hat—and glued them on. My project was now vastly different from everyone else's, achieved just by looking at things a bit differently. That simple lesson changed my perspective on everything. It was a good excuse to start breaking rules.

Your production is sourced from different places. What did you do to find these and make them work for you?

My partner, Adam Kornfield, gets all the credit for this. We split responsibilities in a manner that plays towards our strengths: Adam handles logistics, production, and finance. I handle design, marketing, and community. (Of course, there's also a lot of overlap, considering it's just the two of us.) When it comes to production, Adam is all about it. He's searched the world over for manufacturers, been in contact with people on every continent, and flown literally tens of thousands of miles to bring things to life. People often ask us how we find our manufacturers, and I wish I could give a catchall answer that would make it easy, but that just isn't the case. The answer is exactly what you'd expect: lots of research, trial and error, and persistence. There's quite a bit that happens before we get to manufacturing, as well. First we hack things together in-house. A shitty mockup is a thousand times more useful than an exquisite idea that exists only in your head. Even if the mockup is terrible,

at least it's there in front of you. Now you can start talking about it with others on a more productive level. The very first Confidant prototype was a notebook wrapped in painting canvas. The second prototype was made while sitting in my underwear at the kitchen table on a Saturday morning. Both were hardly perfect, but they got the idea out of my head and onto the table; they became real. After that it was just a matter of refining the book until it felt just right.

Future plans are hush-hush, but can you give a hint of what's going to happen next?

Our mission is singular: to empower thinkers in their journey to create and inspire the world. That leaves a lot of possibility on the table.

Khoi Vinh

THE REALITY OF CREATING A BUSINESS

Khoi Vinh is a pioneer of digital communications. He started his own web journal, Subtraction, and was the design director of the *New York Times* digital before leaving for the insecurity of the start-up world. His first product, Mixel, a collage-making program for kids of all ages, has done well for itself, and Vinh has joined the ranks of the serial entrepreneurs.

You've been engaged in digital entrepreneurship for a number of years. Would you say that Subtraction was your first venture?

Yes, I think that's accurate to say. When I bought the domain name, I didn't really know what I was going to do with it, and in fact it took me a number of years to figure that out. But I knew that it would be a storefront of some kind, a shingle to hang, so to speak, that would represent me as a business of some kind. At first that meant putting my portfolio online, but I also played

with making Subtraction.com a site for a really big, pretend design studio, with lots of staff and a big client list. I enjoyed the idea of a business, of creating all of the collateral and accoutrements of a business, before I even had a business. In fact, that early version of the site was convincing enough that recruiters started contacting me to see if I needed to hire more people.

That iteration didn't last particularly long, though. Eventually I turned Subtraction.com into a blog, and that became a kind of microbusiness of its own. It's not really anything like a "real" publication, but in some ways it has the responsibilities of a publication. I need to publish content regularly, and it brings in a certain amount of revenue through advertising arrangements and products that I sell through it.

My first "real" venture, though, was cofounding the design studio—a real one this time—Behavior. That was a services business, and it was a great experience. My partners and I built a real client list and did some great work. It also taught me how much I really don't like services and working with clients. After four years there, I was exhausted. Coincidentally, the *New York Times* came calling, which was a tremendous opportunity, so I happily set aside my entrepreneurial urges for a while and joined the *Times* for four and a half years.

After leaving the New York Times, *where you were digital design director, you developed your own product for the iPad. How did this come about, what did you do to make it a reality, and what was the response to your efforts?*

I knew that I wanted to do something at the intersection of social software and mobile devices, and so I started thinking about how the iPad was so transformative as a tool for self-expression. I gambled that you could build a robust social network on top of that opportunity that could connect people all over the world to help one another rediscover a child-like creativity that most of us set aside as we enter adulthood.

We called the product Mixel and we launched it about one year after I left the *Times*. The response was very positive; we had a really strong community of users who were very passionate about it.

But at that point I ran headfirst into the reality of creating a business, rather than just a product—or even just an app, which is all we really had. The difference between that and a sustainable enterprise is very, very stark, and I realized that even though we had a great start, we had fundamentally miscalculated the business proposition from the beginning—not just the revenue model, but the way we structured the financing, and the way we thought about the roadmap for the business. It was pretty heartbreaking for me as well as for all the people who had so generously poured their time and passion into the community we had built.

You sold your venture. What was involved with making it available? And what was your responsibility once it sold?

We had been lucky in that the market then was very ripe for large companies acquiring small ones just for their talent—"acqui-hires." We had been getting a lot of inbound interest for that kind of deal, but when we saw the writing on the wall, we started to take them seriously. We talked to a lot of companies; once one was affirmatively interested, it was pretty easy to start similar, brass-tacks conversations with the others.

Eventually we settled on one acquirer who satisfied our main goals: return money to investors, procure equity in the acquiring company for my cofounder and me, secure jobs for all of our employees—and avoid relocating to the Bay Area. We all wanted to stay in New York.

This was a pure talent deal, so while the acquiring company generously allowed us to maintain the Mixel app in the marketplace, the acquisition effectively halted future development on it. Once the deal closed, I reported to the new company for my new job, which was fun at first but, as is typical with many of these deals, was ultimately pretty uncomfortable. It's hard for any company to know what to do with a founder of a company they've acquired; dropping them into middle management is an imperfect solution, but it's usually the only one that the organization knows how to do. I lasted only six months before both the management and I decided it wasn't working, so I was able to leave on good terms.

You obviously have a serial entrepreneurial streak. Tell us about your current venture?

After raising venture capital for Mixel, I learned that it's really not for me, at least not for now. What I crave more than anything is to own my own time and to be my own boss. That's not really the case with venture capital, where your investors and your board are effectively your bosses. Also, after Behavior, then the *Times*, and then Mixel, I found myself exhausted by singularly devoting myself to mammoth projects. Behavior and Mixel, particularly, were all consuming, because I had to build them up from scratch to satisfy very large goals.

Welcome to Khoi & Laura's Kidpost for Mon, Mar 14!

Laura Holder shared this on Facebook
Sunday, March 13 at 11:10 AM

Lorem ipsum dolor sit amet, consectetur adipisicing elit, sed do eiusmod tempor incididunt ut labore et dolore magna aliqua. #kidpost

@khoi posted this on Instagram
Sunday, March 13 at 8:10 AM

#kidpost

So now I'm relishing the ability to work on a number of different things. I have one product that's in development, Kidpost, which is a collaboration with two friends. We're building a very, very sleek and feature limited tool that collects photos and updates that parents post about their young kids, bundles them up into a daily email digest, and sends that digest off to their friends and families. We're trying to make it easier for parents, who want to post to their preferred social networks, to keep their extended families in the loop on how their kids are progressing, without requiring those family and friends to sign up for every network and/or constantly check in.

It's specifically designed to be lightweight and simple enough to build on a part-time basis; we hope to get the "minimum viable product" version into the market-place soon to test the waters. If it's successful, we'll put more muscle into it. If it's not, we'll ditch it, which is an option you don't really get with venture capital. We've bootstrapped this, funding it entirely with our own cash (it's required very little so far) and our own time, so we don't have to answer to anyone else about it.

I also have other projects—a new photography app, a book, a collaboration with Adobe—designed at a similar scale; simple, highly doable projects that get out into the world quickly and that generate revenue immediately (another painful lesson from Mixel, which did not charge). What I'm trying to do is to build mul-tiple revenue streams and a customer base that I can come back to again and again with new products. It's more like a mom-and-pop model than what we think of as a start-up; the venture capital industry somewhat derisively calls these kinds of businesses "lifestyle businesses."

Randy J. Hunt

THE DIGITAL MARKETPLACE

The Creative Director for Etsy, Randy J. Hunt, a graduate of the SVA MFA Design/Designer as Author + Entrepreneur program, is the head of design at Etsy, the online marketplace. His work with a large number of design entrepreneurs gives him unique insight into the process that makers must go through in the digital age.

How do you define entrepreneurship in relation to what you do?

For me, entrepreneurship has two parts: the starting of a business itself, and the spirit and approach of being a person who starts a business. That spirit and approach can be applied in other applications beyond the starting of a business. For me, in my role as the creative director and head of design at Etsy, that's how entrepreneurship applies. Additionally, having been an entrepreneur, I can relate to the experiences and challenges of many members of our community, including:

- *The interaction between recognizing opportunity and being compelled by an idea*
- *The joy and challenges of starting something new*
- *Developing and applying business acumen as a person most well-versed in creative applications*
- *The scrappiness and resourcefulness of bootstrapping a business*

You are also head of design at Etsy. Presumably, this means working with small entrepreneurs. What have you learned from this experience?

We work with many, many entrepreneurs. More than anything, I'm reminded of three things:

- *Those who are enthusiastic about making a viable business are far more likely to do so. Having an ambivalent relationship to business doesn't work. Accept that business can be a creative experience, and you'll enjoy it rather than resent it.*
- *The spirit of generosity and community is huge for helping people learn about and persevere through the challenges of business.*
- *You've got to be open to learning and evolving both your business and yourself. Running a business is an exercise in growth in so many ways. Staying static doesn't tend to work out well.*

Do design and business have to be separate activities?

In short: no. In fact, I find it very difficult for me personally to separate the two. Because I see design, in part, as an approach to problem-solving and decision making, I see business decisions as design problems.

Do you see a relationship between good design and better sales?

It's an interesting question, because there are always counter examples: something that seems like "bad design" but does really well in a commercial sense. This all depends on your definition of "design" and "good design" too. Take the Steve Jobs definition: "Design is how it works." He's really suggesting that design is much deeper than how it looks. Take the Eameses: "The details are the design." Again, they're saying that good design is pretty broad.

With all that in mind, I've seen things that aren't well designed do well in the market . . . but I've seen things that are designed well do better.

What is it about the things that do best?

They're great aesthetic experiences, they work well, they're well made, they're relevant, and they're well promoted.

Is design becoming more of a selling point for the Etsy generation?

Absolutely. For Etsy sellers, they're increasingly concerned about design. For shoppers, they're increasingly design-savvy. This is great for both sides, and there's a natural match on the supply and demand sides.

Does Etsy directly or indirectly advocate design entrepreneurship?

I'd say it's indirect. Etsy almost never uses the term "design entrepreneurship." If your definition is reasonably wide, then pretty much every entrepreneur in the Etsy ecosystem is a design entrepreneur or works with one. As of June 2014, that's 1.2 million active shops. That's a lot of design entrepreneurs! We're advocates for all of them.

Tina Roth Eisenberg

FRONTIER WOMAN ONLINE

Tina Roth Eisenberg, a.k.a. swissmiss, a design impresario by any other name, has over the past several years emerged as a model design entrepreneur. Although her popular swissmiss blog (so named because she is a New York transplant from the Swiss Alps) began as a personal visual archive—and was never intended to be a business—it is a highly trafficked design site that covers all manner of design objects, graphics, products, and film. The turning point came when, a few months into it, a friend asked to see her stats. Huge! The swissmiss blog, which she started in 2005, was always a supplementary reference and integral to her daily routine as a designer. A year later, she started her own design studio in Brooklyn, New York. Then in 2008, she began a small empire: first, CreativeMornings in 2008, a series of early morning talks for the local creative community, reminding them that we are all part of a global ecosystem; TeuxDeux in 2009, a self-help iPhone App; and Tattly in 2011, temporary designer tattoos, which are selling briskly.

How did swissmiss start?

Swissmiss started in 2005 as a personal visual archive. Visual blogging tools like Pinterest and Tumblr weren't invented and I was craving a visual way of keeping track of all my online finds. So, I started a blog for myself, as a visual personal archive. After a few months I checked my stats and noticed that I had a growing readership. It has been growing ever since.

At what point did you see its potential as the basis for a business?

I never intended my blog to become a business. I still don't. I look at it as a labor of love that has organically started generating passive income that has then allowed me to start other side projects, which themselves have turned into businesses (CreativeMornings, Tattly, TeuxDeux). I consider myself an accidental business person.

What were the signs?

I never intended to have ads on my site, but when Jim Coudal of The Deck Network reached out to me and invited me to be part of their network, I couldn't say no. It was such an honor to be included. Once I started generating income from my blog I was able to justify spending more time on it. The ads on my site are subtle, and purposely so. I could have plastered my site with lots of ads and made tons of money. That's not what I believe in. I respect my readers too much for that.

CreativeMornings is a very successful and well-known endeavor. How did you make this work out?

I believe in making things better instead of simply complaining. CreativeMornings is a direct result of that. In 2005 I was craving an easy way for the creative community in NYC to connect. Conferences are great for that, but they are time consuming and expensive. I figured there had to be a regular accessible event that would allow me to mingle with likeminded folks. And that's exactly what we do with

CreativeMornings. Once a month we gather for breakfast and a twenty-minute presentation. For free. The idea has caught on, and we have sixty-five chapters all over the world. CreativeMornings is one of my dearest labors of love and a perfect example of how trust breeds magic. All of our chapter hosts run their local organization on a volunteer basis. I completely trust them and am continuously impressed by what they put together. Every month there are sixty-five CreativeMornings happening all over the world. It's humbling.

Do you think of yourself as an entrepreneur? Do you have any methods for being one?

Yes. Or let's say, I call myself the queen of accidental businesses. I am starting to become more confident in my skills of leading companies and do enjoy it. I tremendously enjoy motivating a team and creating an environment in which my staff can thrive. In my recent Do Lectures talk (http://dolectures.com/lectures/trust-breeds-magic/) I speak quite a bit on how I run my companies and the core principles I base all of my decisions on.

You started Tattly, presumably, on a lark. It's now very big. Are you surprised? What kind of adjustments did you have to make along the way to accommodate this success?

Yes! I started Tattly because I was annoyed with the badly designed and poorly produced temporary tattoos my daughter would bring home. Given that I am a web designer with a big network of talented illustrator friends, it was a no-brainer to go ahead and produce cool tattoos. I imagined that my small design community

would get a kick out of them and was prepared to ship a few dozen tattoos a day. What I didn't expect is that we would end up in stores like J. Crew and museum stores all over the world. We are now a team of ten and ship worldwide out of Brooklyn. We are in over seven hundred stores all over the world. It makes me giddy to think that I have created a product that people love and that makes them smile.

How do you filter your big from your small ideas?

I am a firm believer in trusting your gut instincts. It's a skill that our society is losing more and more. I am doing my best to teach my children to be in tune with their intuition.

Ron Goldin

PRODUCTS IN THE WILD

Ron Goldin is a designer turned entrepreneur. He is the founder and creative director of Akko, a multidisciplinary design studio that provides user experience, design, and strategy services and through which he has developed prototypes for new ventures. A venture enabler, Goldin is the creator of Artifacts salon, where innovators in the arts and new media gather.

Your website states "there's a lot of good ideas out there." How do you know which ones to invest in?

My number one criteria for what I believe are the most successful ideas are those that clearly solve real-world problems. This sounds obvious, but there are many products out there that are either recombinations and mashups of already successful products or technology for technology's sake. When you a see a real-world behavior and identify a way that a product can make that behavior better—easier, faster, more delightful—that's a great starting point. Sometimes formal or informal research— talking to people about how product ideas fit into their lives by understanding their pain points and needs—has helped me to identify what the highest-value products might be versus the nice-to-haves. Other times, and very common in the start-up world, creating a prototype and putting it out into the wild to see if it sticks can be the most objective way to try out an idea without investing too much time and energy down the wrong path.

How does design fit into your entrepreneurial plans?

I was definitely a designer and technologist before I was an entrepreneur. I studied a combination of traditional design, psychology, and computer science, and only when I graduated and worked for a number of years did I learn the potential of interaction design and user experience as a leadership role in organizations. I found myself doing a lot of synthesis in those roles—taking lots of perspectives, from design to technology to marketing and business requirements, and somehow coming out of that cacophony with a perspective that was customer-driven, good for the business, and feasible. Since running my own agency, Studio Akko (http://akko.co), I've had a chance to take on start-ups as well as bigger companies. Working with founders of bleeding-edge companies that are putting their hearts and souls into an idea they believe in has definitely inspired me to take incubating my own product ideas more seriously. I think designers are great at figuring out how to get things done in a clever way with limited resources, and I'm excited to see more designers take the leap into the entrepreneur's seat.

Can you define and describe your Homebrew'd Projects?

Homebrew'd Projects are my studio's attempt to identify and solve problems we see in our own lives or the world around us, rather than being given a brief by clients. Some of the Homebrew'd Projects are conceptual ideas and some are actual Minimum Viable Products (MVPs, in the start-up world) that we put out into the wild and

*River Road are industrial design renderings
by Greg MacNamara, owner of Formant Studios,
in collaboration with Studio Akko, on the creation of BKIN.*

see if they stick. One conceptual product is BKIN, which is a wayfinding system for remote places like national forests and backcountry ski slopes. It's a solar-powered device with a small footprint and minimal installation requirements. It lives outdoors, allowing people to interact with a digital map and discover both nearby attractions and hazards as well as communicate to a central station in emergency scenarios. It came out of what felt like a near-death experience where I got caught after closing hours on the wrong side of a ski slope as it was getting dark with no cell reception. I was lucky that some security guard checking the grounds happened to find me and help me back to civilization. I left that situation thinking this was a solvable problem, how to stay in the know in places that are outside of the reach of technology. A few weeks later, a brainstorm with an industrial designer spawned the idea for BKIN, a product that works anywhere and anytime and handles both emergency communication and digital wayfinding.

What distinguishes them from other ventures?

The biggest thing is that with Homebrew'd Projects, there are no clients. While that may mean unlimited freedom, that also means the product can go in a million different directions and it's up to us to determine what the goals, criteria for success, and outcomes are. That said, with little between us and design, the products can be concepted extremely quickly and efficiently. As long as the vision for who and what it's for is crisp and clear, the design follows pretty naturally. We love these kinds of projects because they also allow us to really take risks where failure is painless. Another big part of Homebrew'd Projects is stretching beyond your discipline. BKIN was a close collaboration with an industrial designer outside of our team to help render

The audience at an "Artifacts" event using 3D glasses to watch Ben Vershbow, Lab Manager for the NY Public Library Labs, demo a collection of online archived stereographic images of historical sites in New York City.

A custom rubber stamp used to create "trading cards" to help people learn the presenters. The card helped people meet strangers through a series of games.

images of what it could look like and feel like from a physical standpoint, while we handled research and software requirements, as well as detailed interaction and visual design for the interface. I actually founded an event called Artifacts (http://akko.co/artifacts) specifically to foster a community of creatives, entrepreneurs, and technologists both inside and outside of tech in order to spawn cross-disciplinary collaborations for both our studio and others. It's created a number of serendipitous creative connections that will hopefully result in some great products someday soon.

Do you have a long-term strategy for how to make and put products into the market?

It's a really exciting time because I feel like there are more options than ever before for someone with an idea to get something made. Manufacturing and rapid prototyping are cheaper and easier than ever. Services like Quirky are a powerful way to take the mystery of manufacturing and allow anyone with an idea to find an audience and get something built. Putting things out into the market, however, is still one of the biggest barriers to entrepreneurs as it requires many moving parts, from branding, marketing, and promotion to sales and partnerships. My advice to others and the advice I give myself is find someone stronger than you are in those areas—perhaps with an MBA—to partner with once you get to that phase of product

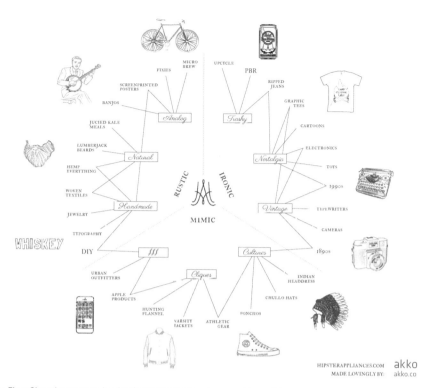

The Flow Chart is a tongue-in-cheek graphic design piece used to explain the "origins of the hipster aesthetic." (See hipsterappliances.com.)

maturity. In general, the strongest entrepreneurs realize that they don't have to be experts at everything. Knowing what you don't know and finding people that can fill in the gaps in your own weakness are sometimes what make or break a successful product endeavor. Again, Artifacts the event series is really meant for us to foster a community of people passionate about making things with a vast array of skill sets so you can find people to go to when you've got a great idea and need a partner or some specific type of support.

What are some of the challenges you've encountered?

Funding is probably the biggest challenge for most entrepreneurs. In the start-up world, there's a whole range, from angel investors to venture capitalists, who are as passionate as entrepreneurs about problem solving. Working with them is not only a great way to get to the resources you need but also to have a network of advisors that can walk you through the common problems that ALL businesses have, such as scaling up. Depending on the idea, I still think starting scrappy and making a pilot or prototype to test the waters is a smarter tactic than building your full-blown masterpiece from the get-go, and services like Kickstarter are a great way for people to bypass traditional fundraising and get some seed money while also building buzz for their idea. I've been struggling with how to balance my consulting work with dedicating time and resources to building products, and diverting attention to new ideas while growing the business is a tricky balancing act.

Have you had any failures, and if yes, how did you overcome them?

Last year, I had a product idea that I was (and still am) extremely excited about. Thinking like a start-up, I set up a far too aggressive deadline in the spirit of being lean and agile. I was frustrated with the billable projects that were distracting me from working on this passion project, and eventually I started becoming frustrated with the project itself. One thing led to the other, and I had to eventually put it to rest for a few months while I became engulfed in my studio work. There's a principle I recall reading in Mikhaly Csikszentmihalyi's book *Flow* years ago, which talks about how sometimes an idea can still "incubate" in your mind even while you're not actively attending to it. I think this is exactly what happened. Over the course of those few months, I started noticing things in the world that helped to validate, refine, and question some of my assumptions about this product. When I finally picked the project back up again to do some sketching, the goal and the approach for the product felt different—they were actually more focused and refined.

What are your most satisfying outcomes?

My most satisfying outcome is not about the product itself but about the process in which the team and I built the product. My team and I at Akko once made a product in a few weeks, which started out as an inside joke. We had a coffee maker in one of our offices that was the most ridiculously over-designed piece of machinery I've ever seen. We wanted to hate the thing because it was so complicated to use, but it

made such incredibly good coffee. I said something to the effect of "There should be a website where people can find products they want to hate but kind of love." A few cups of coffee later and some hilarious brainstorming ended in us buying the domain hipsterappliances.com. We then created an online aggregator for obscure seasonal products inspired by "discerning subcultures" (a.k.a. hipsters). We sketched a logo, designed the pages, and used a rapid prototyping tool to make a website for it in a day and pushed it live. We got thousands of hits on the first day. More importantly, it was a great feeling to see the whole team rally behind an idea out of sheer curiosity to see what would come of it and how the world would react to it.

Celia Cheng

A DIGITAL FEAST

Cravings started when, as a student in the SVA MFA Design/Designer as Author + Entrepreneur program in 2005, Celia developed a guide to finding specific dishes in restaurants. Over the ensuing years it evolved into a design-conscious online publication that highlights food, wine, travel, and lifestyle. To make it more expandable, Cheng founded Cravings Productions, which produces videos, custom letterpress, photography, design, and consulting services. Now she travels between New York, Taiwan, Hawaii, and Japan.

You left a good job to start Cravings. Why and how?

Cravings brought out the entrepreneur in me. What started out as a database of recommended dishes at restaurants soon grew to include events to meet and eat with chefs, sweepstakes giveaways, and travel videos. The creative ideas just kept pouring out and I was having so much fun with it, the growth was organic. Two years after findyourcraving.com launched, I quit my job to focus on it full time. My timing was just right, since blogging, food culture, and social media were all experiencing explosive growth.

What triggered your interest in developing Cravings?

I saw a need in the marketplace. I was getting so many inquiries on where to eat and drink, and what to order, that I realized I needed to create a guide that could be easily accessed by a large audience. Print-version Zagat guides were still in their heyday back then, but I knew that this tool I was creating needed to be online. Being online allowed us to expand quickly from a food guide to a lifestyle guide extending to topics on wines, champagnes, travel, and culture. I also knew that Cravings needed to be colorful, lively, and luscious, just as food should be, and as a designer, I could make my guide unique by incorporating design, creativity, and fun. One of the main aspects that differentiates Cravings from other guides is that we are just as focused on the design as we are on the content. I am both a food editor and a graphic designer, and I find gastronomy and design to be completely complementary, and what sets us apart.

How have you gone about making it into a business?

A combination of online advertising, partnerships, organizing events, and providing consulting, video production, and graphic design services. Cravings focuses on food, wine, travel, and lifestyle, all of which is presented through thoughtful design. People noticed the design immediately and started to ask us to help them with design services from the beginning. As the demand for these different revenue streams grew, I decided to pull them together and launch Cravings Productions, a company that produces videos and provides letterpress, design services, and photography, with a focus on the food and beverage industry.

Have your plans and goals always worked out the way you want? Were there failures, and how did you overcome them? What did you learn from them?

SUSHI NAKAMURA 鮨 なかむら

AJI SUSHI

f SHARE
p PIN IT
y TWEET
✉ EMAIL
⚑ FLAG
★ FAVE

MY FAVORITES

[-] Information

SUSHI NAKAMURA 鮨 なかむら

7-17-16 Roppongi, Minato-ku
Tokyo, 106-0032, Japan
+81-(0)3-3746-0856

Aji Sushi: $$$$

SEE ALL CRAVINGS IN ROPPONGI (5)

YOU MIGHT ALSO LIKE...

FEATURED IN...

Masanori Nakamura's Michelin-starred sushi bar is a honey-hued cocoon designed, like many other sushi restaurants of its kind, to soothe the senses and focus the taste buds. After one bite of the chef's exquisite sushi you'll know you're in the hands of a master. One standout was his *aji* (horse mackerel) sushi. Part of the pleasure is watching Nakamura score (with lightning speed) the top of the fish *tateyoko* (horizontally and vertically). When it is draped over a dainty finger of vinegared rice from Niigata Prefecture, a bumpy cross-hatch pattern of silver and pink emerges. The technique renders the fish delectably silky. No vulgar soy sauce needed here; Nakamura brushes the top of the sushi with a layer of subtle *nikiri*, a soy sauce and sake mixture in which the sake has been cooked off. Be prepared for the exotic, too: our omakase included abalone dressed with the intestines of sea cucumber and an intensely salty, flavorful taste of fermented red sea urchin.

Editor's Pick   Nancy Matsumoto | August 15, 2013

There have been lots of curveballs along the way and I expect many more to come. Some partnerships didn't work out the way we envisioned and some streams of content didn't appeal to our audience, but the good thing is that we learn from each lesson and don't put ourselves in the same situation. It's extremely important whom you choose to work with: your team, your partners, your vendors. I've learned to listen to feedback from my team and my audience, and always strive to exceed my standards.

You were putting on events. Is that still part of your business plan?

If the right opportunity comes along, we are open to putting on events, but it's not part of our core business right now.

Can you actually profit from a website newsletter? How?

The newsletter is part of the brand outreach to our community. It's a platform that keeps our subscribers in the loop of what we are up to. The content we provide attracts an audience that has genuine interest in our recommendations. In addition to our latest content updates, the newsletter also lets our community know when we have events or sell services or products.

The digital space is the Wild West of business. Have you figured out how to tame it?

At the digital agency I worked at before Cravings, we used to joke, "Phil, so did you reach the end of the Internet today?" It may seem odd that we had a dedicated resource whose job was to surf the web, but as much as it seems like it is play, it's really work. Keeping up with the digital space and finding new trends, strange phenomena, emerging technologies, and more is work, and it's endless. There are no limits to the opportunities in the digital frontier. Technology is not something we can tame, because it is constantly changing, but it's a matter of figuring out which tools can be useful to your business. For example, when we launched Cravings, we focused more on colors and used photos sparingly, due to the high cost of setting up photo shoots. While we started investing in photography equipment and honing our skills, smartphones proliferated and photographing food became so easy. Similarly, YouTube opened the gates for video blogging, and today, video content is just as common as written content. Once we jumped on that technology, it opened new doors for us both in terms of a new audience—our viewer demographic on YouTube is very different from that of our website visitors—and a new revenue stream. Once people saw our videos and knew we could make short, creative, and well-edited videos, they started asking for the service, and now videos are a growing market. Social media completely changed the landscape, allowing you to reach an audience by just putting it out there. It's spurred the growth of artisanal producers, who once had to worry about how to market and distribute their homegrown product but now can easily reach millions of people. In that same vein, while letterpress seems like an old-school art form, it's one of the design services we provide, and by promoting it via social media, it became an instant business. Tomorrow there will be something new, and I look forward to seeing how it will fit into my business.

Eric Zimmerman

GAMES FOR A LIVING

Eric Zimmerman plays games for a living. He also makes games and teaches game design. He was an early proponent of thinking persons' gaming. His business, Gamelab, a computer game development company based in Manhattan, gave him the experience in working with clients, partners, and others, while retaining freedom to pursue his own ideas. Every year he hosts the Game Design Challenge at the Game Developers Conference.

You are one of the pioneer games-persons. How did you decide on this entrepreneurial path?

It turns out that I have liked games my whole life—not just playing games, but making them too. I spent a lot of my childhood creating variations on kick the can, inventing rules for plastic army men battles, and designing my own board games. I studied art right around the turn of the 1990s, and I was looking for a cultural form that was doing something genuinely new. It turned out to be video games, which felt like a kind of culture that was undergoing radical evolution. So I became a game designer in my search for a cultural form that was breaking new ground. At the same time, I was also returning to a childhood passion.

At what point did you turn from working for others to being your own business?

I started my studio, Gamelab, in 2000 (with game designer Peter Lee) after working in the industry for about six years. So I already knew a lot about how the games business worked. However, starting a business doesn't mean you are not working for other people! We had clients, partners, and publishers, and while we did original work, we were never absolutely free of working for others. Things are different today. With the rise of digital distribution, independent games have blossomed, and it is possible for a very small business to make games and sell them directly to a large audience. That wasn't possible when we started Gamelab. So much has changed in just a few years!

Do you hire yourself out to produce proprietary games for others?

Since closing Gamelab in 2009, I did some freelance work on my own for a few years. Today, however, I am a full-time professor at the NYU Game Center. So in addition to teaching, my design work now focuses exclusively on personal projects. Perhaps I will return again to freelance consulting and design, but I am happy where I am right now.

Your games are not the conventional kind. You push the boundaries. Is this a profitable space for you?

Yes and no. Some of my games, such as the large-scale physical game installations I have created with architect Nathalie Pozzi, are art projects that do not have any kind of profit. Other games I make, such as the card game Metagame that I designed with Colleen Macklin and John Sharp through our design collective Local No. 12, are commercial products that are sold for a profit. I like being able to do both commercial and noncommercial work—both have important kinds of design constraints.

Do you keep ownership of your games?

Because I am no longer doing freelance work-for-hire, I do maintain ownership of most of my projects. Sometimes, when there is a publisher involved—such as my board game Quantum that was published by Fun-Forge—the publisher has publishing rights. But I retain ownership and control over the intellectual property. Another project of mine, SiSSYFiGHT 2000, an online game about little girls fighting on a playground, was just released as open source. So in that case, the game has become public domain intellectual property, and in a sense everyone can own it and do with it whatever they want. It's nice to be exploring these different permutations of intellectual property ownership.

What are your most satisfying moments as an entrepreneur?

The sweetest pleasure of game design for me is when I see a player doing things with my games that I never could have anticipated in advance. For me, games are less like traditional forms of art or beautiful objects designed for contemplation. They are more like toolboxes—objects that players use to do things and make things. So every time players play one of my games, it is an opportunity for me to see something new.

What do you think makes your method different from others?

I focus very heavily on iterative design—in fact, I am sometimes called a "playtesting fundamentalist" because I believe very strongly in rapid prototyping and constant testing with players. Game design sits right on the border between more functional design disciplines like graphic design, industrial design, and architecture—and art and entertainment, which have very little utilitarian function. Other game designers think of themselves more as artists, and shy away from playtesting, but I fall more on

the designer side of the equation. Both approaches are fine, depending on how you work and what you are trying to do.

You must have had failures. What did you learn from them?

I fail early and often. Part of my emphasis on iterative design is that it allows for failure as part of the process. I am also continually dissatisfied with my own work. For me, this dissatisfaction is part of the creative urge. If I ever felt like I did something that was somehow an actual "success," I'm not sure why I would keep going.

Albert Pereta

BEING ACQUIRED TO BE HIRED

Albert Pereta is a lead product designer at Pinterest and creative entrepreneur. Cofounder of Icebergs (acquired by Pinterest), MareMae, Wiselist, and Dear Barcelona. He was born in Barcelona and moved to New York to graduate from the SVA MFA Design/Designer as Author + Entrepreneur program. Currently living in San Francisco, Pereta discusses how his venture became acquired by Pinterest.

How and why was Icebergs conceived?

Icebergs was born as a thesis project at SVA. After watching how difficult it was for my fellow creatives to keep their projects, inspiration, and research organized, I decided that I wanted to build something that could make their lives easier. I built a small prototype and put up a landing page for interested people to sign up. The interest was overwhelming.

Briefly explain the purpose of Icebergs?

Icebergs was a visual organization app for creative minds. We're always doing research and starting new projects, but it's easy to get overwhelmed with your own content after a while. I wanted to create a private space in the cloud for people to save anything from the web, upload files, write notes, and collaborate with all the content seamlessly.

After grad school, how did you go about developing Icebergs?

I moved back to Barcelona and I partnered with a business cofounder. We raised some money from family and friends, hired a developer, and built an MVP (Minimum Viable Product) in less than four months. Once the first signup page was up,

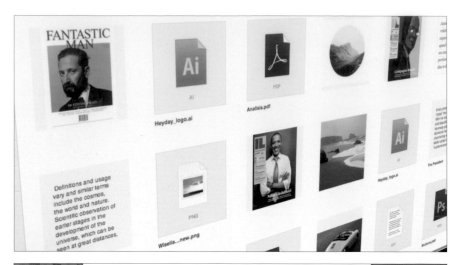

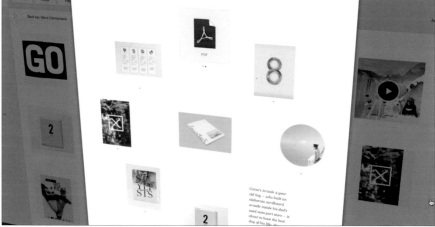

we shared it on our social media networks, and it went viral. We had a waiting list of ten thousand people in two weeks.

What was the outcome of your efforts to make Icebergs real?

Building a business is probably the most difficult thing I've ever done. Adding that the business was a tech start-up made things ten times crazier and faster. You learn to live with uncertainty and absolute chaos. You commit your whole being to this venture, and you need to be determined. When we created Icebergs, it was our first company and we never knew what the outcome would be, but we were sure that we were onto something and that we just had to build it. Two years later, here we are, working in one of the most promising start-ups of Silicon Valley and still trying to change the world.

How was Pinterest involved?

Pinterest noticed Icebergs a few months after our launch. We were starting to gain traction, and we kept in touch along the way.

When they decided to take it on, what did they offer?

After a year and a half, we proved what we could do with Icebergs, and the conversations with Pinterest gained momentum. Icebergs was acquired by Pinterest, and both founders were moved to San Francisco to join their talented team. Now here we are, and the future looks really promising.

Do you feel good about your dealings?

Couldn't be happier. We joined a team of word-class talent, and the level of work we do is astonishing. I'm always learning and growing as a professional. I'm seeing how a small start-up becomes a top company, and that's valuable. Everything I see and learn will allow me to be better at any other venture.

What is your status now?

I'm a lead product designer at Pinterest. I work on new products from concept to visuals to shipping. I also cofounded two new ventures back in Europe: a premium Dead Sea cosmetics brand called MareMae, and a line of quality city guides made by locals called Dear Barcelona.

Do you see Icebergs as an entity/venture or a stepping-stone?

Icebergs as a company was closed. The idea was to take what we learned and what people loved about Icebergs and apply it to Pinterest and make it our own. I learned a lot and I still keep learning from it. I'm absolutely sure that this experience will shape my future ventures and upcoming new projects in unexpected ways. Can't wait to see what's next!

Cary Murnion and Jonathan Millet

MAKING COOTIES

Cary Murnion and directing partner Jonathan Millet have always been interested in directing film. They idolized Mike Mills, who made the transition from graphic designer to filmmaker in a very successful way, so they knew it could be done. In 2004, Nike approached the duo and gave them the opportunity to write, produce, and direct a short film as part of their film series *The Art of Speed*. That led to them directing more live-action short films with Nike and other brands as well as TV commercials. Essentially, they went to an on-the-job film school that was funded by their clients. Now *Cooties*, their first feature, is ready for its close-up.

You've been essentially a graphic design firm. How did the film Cooties, *a disease that takes over an elementary school, take shape?*

In 2009 a film production company, Blowtorch, approached us because they were funding a series of short films to play before their feature-length movies. There was no brand attached, so that's when we made our R-rated short film, *Boob*. It's the story of a boob that comes alive and terrorizes the people in a hospital as it tries to escape, but not before it falls in love with a sexy nurse.

Boob went to South by Southwest, attracting some attention in the industry. It was passed along to the producers of *Cooties*, who were looking for a director. *Boob* had a similar mix of comedy and horror as *Cooties* did, making us a good match. The producers contacted us, and we went to Los Angeles to pitch our directorial approach. They loved our vision and brought us on board when they secured financing in May 2013. We filmed the movie over twenty-five days between July and August.

While working on this project, were graphic design and studio work put on hiatus?

Not at all. We had multiple projects going on at the studio while we were directing the movie. We have a great team who handled the studio work, allowing Jon and me to devote our full attention to the film. We had been doing this on a smaller scale when we'd direct the commercials and short films, so it wasn't completely foreign to the way our studio works.

What was the process of conceiving, creating, directing, and producing Cooties *to make it a viable property?*

Well, first off, *Cooties* is not our idea. The basic story was conceived by Josh Waller, who's one of the producers of the film, along with his partners, Elijah Wood and Daniel Noah. The script was written by Leigh Whannell, who created the *Saw* and *Insidious* franchises, and Ian Brennan, who, along with Ryan Murphy, created *Glee*. So you can get a feel for the tone of the script if you mash *Saw* and *Glee* together.

When we were brought on board, we started bringing the movie from the pages of the script into the real world. Explaining what a director does can be confusing to people not involved with the industry since we don't hold the camera or act. In a way it's a lot like a being a designer, whose role can also confuse people out of the industry, who often ask, "Are you an illustrator or a photographer?" In our minds the designer is a director in many ways, since every decision and detail is led by both. The most important starting point is finding the theme, sub-themes, tone, character arcs, story arcs, visual style, and overall approach.

Once those larger aspects are nailed down, every decision is driven by or follows them. So that includes storyboarding, art directing, hiring a crew, casting, finding locations, designing wardrobes, creating hairstyles and practical makeup, working with stunt coordinators to conceive fight sequences, designing weapons that could be made from things that would be found in a grade school basement, all the way through all the post-production aspects like editing, music, sound effects, digital effects, sound mixing, and color correcting. There is a lot of fun work to do as a director, and we loved every minute of it. The way we approached the movie was always with the goal that it could play in big theaters to a wide audience. We wanted to draw them in with laughter and then surprise them with some big scares.

You took it to Sundance, which is no mean feat, and it was picked up by Lionsgate, a major distributor. What did they see in the film to make it ready for prime time?

I think they saw a film that was an original approach to the zombie/monster genre. There have been lots of films and TV shows that fit into this genre, but the ones that have been successful put a unique spin on it, whether it be *The Walking Dead*, *Zombieland*, or *Warm Bodies*. *Cooties* is one of those ideas that makes you ask, "Hasn't that been done before?" *Cooties* seems so obvious in hindsight, but somehow it's never been done till now. It also has an amazing cast who will bring in an audience that might not normally be interested in a film like this. We also like to think that we had a big part in Lionsgate's interest in the film. We were able to walk that fine line between delivering stomach-hurting laughs, while still keeping it grounded enough to deliver real scares and emotional moments. These kinds of elements are what people go to theaters for these days, to laugh and scream together.

You got some fantastic cast members for this comic horror film. How did this happen for two relatively new directors?

Elijah Wood is a producer on this film, and he was attached to play the main character, Clint. So having him on board, and having the great script that Leigh and Ian wrote, helped get a lot of the other actors interested in the film. It was an interesting part of the process, since the director usually does casting and is clearly in charge of these choices, but in this case it was clear we were also being evaluated. One of the ways we won the pitch was creating an extensive look book to clearly express our vision of the film. This helped show our clarity of direction. We also met with each cast member to make sure we were on the same page. We had to make them feel comfortable coming on board with us, while at the same time we were interviewing them to make sure our needs could be met. We were very fortunate to get such a talented and eclectic cast. If anyone ever thinks an actor's job is easy, they should go to a film set. Not only do actors have to be able to turn on their emotions at will, they also have to be able to repeat the process more times than you can ever imagine, for coverage.

What did you have to learn to be directors?

Directing is a strange thing, because you don't necessarily do something specific. You don't have to be an actor, cinematographer, producer, art director, editor, wardrobe designer, or stunt man, but you have to have a deep understanding of everything. For example, a great cinematographer will add a lot to the visuals of the film, but the director has to tell him where to put the camera and how to move it. It's the director who says to shoot a close-up of the hands instead of the face.

The director should also know how different lenses will affect each shot. This doesn't mean the director has to be a good cinematographer, but if he doesn't know the difference between a wide lens and a telephoto lens, his options are detrimentally limited. With a professional and creative cast and crew, the director's job becomes easier. Being a good director means balancing being very confident in yourself with welcoming collaboration from others. What's so fun about being directors is that you get to dip your toe into so many different disciplines, which in turn you're expected to have very definitive opinions on. Yet it's the times you find an opportunity to include someone else's opinion that will inevitably save the film.

What from graphic design could be used in your directorial toolkit?

Graphic designers are directors, which is why they are called art directors or creative directors. Being a graphic designer trained us to be a jacks-of-all-trades. Designers work with all types of artists, writers, marketers, and clients. The designer combines many different puzzle pieces to communicate a certain message. That's what directors do with a film, this aspect of communicating to create. From rough sketch to final product, whether it's a designer explaining an idea to a client or executing an idea through discussions with a programmer, there are many crossovers with a film director.

From a visual standpoint, we feel that being graphic designers greatly enhanced our ability to plan and execute unique scenes in collaboration with our cinematographer. Not to mention we designed and animated the whole opening title sequence to *Cooties*. Not many directors can do that unless they have some background in graphic design.

Despite your impressive new credit, are you still graphic designers?

Yes, definitely, we'll always be graphic designers. We just get restless and like to try new things and find different outlets to express our ideas. Maybe next we'll want to express ourselves through knitting.

Is there another film in the offing?

Yes, at the moment we're working on developing a film based on our own original idea. A few writers are helping us write the script. We're about to shoot a five-minute sample scene to show with the script as a way to secure funding for the feature. We hope to shoot in the summer. We're also starting another script from a completely different idea. We've been meeting with various studios and production companies to see what scripts they have that we feel passionate about. Lots of great opportunities have come from people watching the film at Sundance and really liking it. All this on top of still designing and directing commercials and working on studio projects.

Gael Towey

VISUAL STORYTELLER

Gael Towey's great love is visual storytelling, which is obvious from her series *Portraits in Creativity*, short video sketches about artists and makers, which she produces and directs. (http://gaeltowey.com) Towey was founding design director of *Martha Stewart Living* in 1990 and eventually launched five other lifestyle magazines. Towey became chief creative officer in 2005, overseeing the publishing, merchandising, and Internet segments of the company's design and creative teams. She was also appointed acting editor in chief in 2009. Before leaving Martha Stewart Living Omnimedia, she spearheaded the Martha Stewart American Made Awards for creative entrepreneurship in small business. Her Instagram posts, a complement to her videos, have over 3,000 loyal followers.

Your films seem to be the next step in the evolution that began at Martha Stewart: fine artisans working in unique ways. What made you shift gears from print to video?

Art directing stories for *Martha Stewart Living* was a wonderful experience that put me in touch with artists and growers and craftspeople all over the country. I loved being able to tell their stories. So today I am endeavoring to translate those twenty-plus years of experience as a creative director and editor into moving stories that allow us to hear the artists' voices as they tell their stories. Video is immediate, and it can be as visually beautiful as a print story. I looked for subjects that were seductive and lush in imagery. I wanted to tell the story about how artists take risks and push themselves toward discovery and change. I was hoping that the viewer would feel like they were on that journey with the artist, which is why we tried to capture the sights and sounds of the studio. Working hands and the mess of creativity in action is a seductive and a great way to learn.

I have put together very small teams to produce and direct these videos, and the process of shooting and editing a minidocumentary has been very instructive. Each video is shot by a different cinematographer, and they each have their own style: the amazing photographers Gentl and Hyers shot the Gabriella Kiss video, and we used both stills and video to create the final edit. This gave the piece a distinctive, beautifully composed style that really suited Gabriella's personality. Joe Tomcho shot and edited the Alabama Chanin video, and we traveled to Alabama together, focusing on the feeling of the landscape and the natural beauty of the place that inspired Natalie to go home ten years ago and start her business. Sheila Berger was shot by Philip Lehman, a young man I discovered at RISD who grew up in video, not photography, so his style is more about movement, and he has a bit more of a New York vibe. I hired composers to create an original score for each short film, giving each its own personality and emotional range.

What is your goal with these pieces? Do you simply want to expose your subjects' talents to the world, or is there a larger media plan?

My goal is to find clients who would like to work with me on this kind of video. These videos serve as a snapshot of my interests and the direction I would like to take in my work. I am hoping that people who need this type of video will want to collaborate with me in the future.

My media plan is to expose the videos to as large an audience as possible using social media and reaching out to the many friends I have made in my twenty-plus years as a creative director. I have used Instagram and Twitter, and I have been picked up by a few blogs. It seems to be working; we have had thousands of views in just two weeks.

You focus on creativity and process. How do you select your subjects?

You will notice that my subjects are all experienced; they have been working in their respective fields for twenty or thirty years, and they have the confidence to be risk takers. I believe that artists are comfortable saying, "I don't know where this will

take me," but I am following my instinct and using my craftsmanship and knowledge of materials to investigate and discover a direction. I know or knew of all my subjects, and when I approached them, I felt that they trusted me to tell their story with empathy because of my reputation guiding the Martha Stewart brand for so many years. These are women I greatly admire; they are articulate and focused on excellence. Their work is very beautiful, and the visual nature of the work itself and the way the work is made gave us an opportunity to make the videos visually rich and seductive. All three of the women whom I made films on and the two women whose films I am working on now are in transition, and they are doing something new that they have not done before. Sheila is preparing for her next gallery show, Natalie has just started a new business using her organic cotton to make machine-made garments while continuing her handmade business, and Gabriella just collaborated with her husband of twenty-seven years to make furniture after thirty years as a jewelry designer.

What's planned in the immediate future?

I am continuing to create short videos for clients. I have found a wonderful production studio to partner with me on two long-form documentaries. In both cases I am working directly with the artists. I love the research phase of developing treatments that show the arc of the artists' stories. We are also shooting and editing trailers to pitch to investors.

Aleksandar Maćašev

NANO BLOGGING

Aleksandar Maćašev founded Chromapost as a nano-blogging platform for expressing emotions through color. From that he built up the Chromapost Social Network. What began as an art project naturally evolved into a more universal network replete with a line of product ancillaries, including messenger bags. As a reminder of the significance of color, Chromapost is designed to help users relate to and interface with color as a commercial and emotive aspect of life.

What triggered the idea for Chromapost?

I was frustrated by my uptightness in the usage of color in my art and design practice. We constantly face a torrent of influences on our perception of color and on our expression with color. Culture, visual communication, commerce, and design trends, to name a few, all shape how we think about color. And if you went to an art school, then add color theory to the mix. I wanted to get rid of all these limitations as much as I could and try to use color in a very personal way by expressing my own emotions through it. It's not a very novel idea, but I thought the expression of color had gotten buried under pleasant design color schemes, colors of the season, and such.

Did you consider the commercial potential of this, or was it an artistic impulse?

Initially, it was a personal artistic exercise. I'm very fond of the diary/blog format in art, so I decided to start a blog where each post would be just a single color picked by the common color picker, and that color would summarize my entire daily emotional experience. After a year or two of playing with my color archive and creating some outgrowths out of it, the commercial potentials presented themselves.

Social media is a hot spot (some say a bubble) for creative start-ups. Did you develop a business plan and strategy for Chromapost?

I usually invent as I go and play it by ear. I consider the business side of the project to be an integral part of the creative process. It is not something I add on to the final product. It's a part of the product. And I find it's similar to the "perpetual beta" logic of Internet start-ups.

What are Chromapost's key features?

I don't have key features as much as fluid outlines. Chromapost is being developed on two tracks. The older one, which is my personal art project at www.chromapost.com is a great playground and a testing lab. There have been many art outgrowths based on the idea of compiling a sequence of my daily color posts into an artwork that serves as an emotional footprint of a time period in the same way that the single color is an emotional footprint of my day. The outgrowths range from small digital graphics to outdoor installations the length of an entire city block. Chromapost outdoor installation presented by ArtBridge has been recycled into bags by Brooklyn Industries, which is the first commercial venture. Generally what comes out of this track is within the realm of art.

Chromapost Social Network at www.chromapost.net started one year ago. It was a logical step to make a platform for others to participate. I expanded it with a couple of additional features, like color messaging, Chromapost of the moment, and a Make Art wizard. I find that the Make Art feature has a lot of potential. Basically, users can create artwork out of their own emotional color diary by using templates I created. The aim is to enable everybody to create art. Similar to the logic of Instagram, where everybody can snap a cool picture.

What does Chromapost offer the user that other daily social media does not?

There are two ideas that I found appealing while developing the project: information compression and communicating emotions.

Chromapost tries to go even beyond Twitter's microblogging in 140 characters by using a single color. That's why I like to call it a nanoblogging platform. That simple piece of information is charged with meaning. It's almost like a zip file or a monochrome painting. It looks very simple, but after the second look it bursts with information.

Being cultural animals, our online communication is based on the exchange of quite cerebral pieces of information (text, image, video, sound). Communicating emotions is restricted to emoticons and occasional textual elaborations. We express and exchange, often unconsciously, much better in person. So I find expressing emotions to be a quite uncharted and unexploited land in online communication. People usually shy away from expressing emotions online unless they are extreme. Doing it with color gives you a bit of a safety buffer.

How are you getting the word out to the public?

The project is Internet based, so the usual online channels have worked pretty well so far. The embedded "shareability" of the content also helps the word to get around. Regardless, offline/analog communications also help a lot.

What has been the response from your audience?

People like color. This might sound as absurd as "People like shapes," but it's true. Color is an indivisible part of visual perception. If we see, we see color. The audience and users really enjoy seeing color as emotional information, especially unusual combinations of color that are produced from these emotional colored footprints. There is this primordial, almost childlike pure enjoyment relieved of rules and trends. It confirms my only rule: there are no such things as mismatching colors.

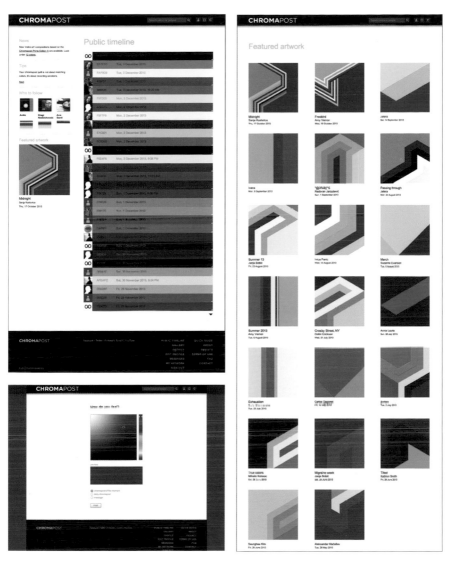

In fact, who is your audience?

The audience for my personal color diary and its outgrowths (www.chromapost.com) has been mainly art/design lovers. That was the initial pool of users of the social network too, but as it has started to spread, there have also been many people outside of art/design circles. I find their engagement and response very enriching. The project is so simple that anybody can use it. Everybody can express their emotions through color and make art out of them.

Have you determined a way to monetize this?

As for chromapost.com, monetizing is mainly in the realm of making art or design products out of my own color diary. With chromapost.net I would like to avoid the usual route of overselling our users' space to advertisers. I see more a platform for users

135

to materialize their artwork, like printing and framing it or putting a unique composition on a carefully selected design product, like a mug, T-shirt, mouse pad or coaster. I don't want to produce cheap sellout stuff, but I also want to make it affordable and attractive to create art. Such a dance on the edge always needs a lot of fine-tuning.

Should social media sites be wells of riches?

I definitely see them as something that is enriching our online experience enormously. On the other hand we have these social media behemoths that take up a lot of space, leaving little room for small businesses to navigate. The deal is to carve out your own space somehow and see if the idea will survive.

What is your next move with Chromapost?

The focus will be on the Make Art feature, offering users more artistic freedom but still guiding them enough so the final result remains good and true to the project. It will probably go in the direction of a generative art platform. I'm also trying to develop a mechanism of making actual products out of these artworks that users can create and purchase. After that I would like to implement geo-tagging. It would be interesting to see color expression on the world map.

Do you see yourself as a design entrepreneur?

For the past ten years, I have been working as a freelance designer and a visual artist, so entrepreneurship is very much part of what I do. It's a very perilous road that requires a lot of creative thinking, not just in doing it, but also in managing it. This is pretty much my only option, since I'm not capable of going back to work in design-office cages. And I certainly don't want to create a cage for others.

Aaron Perry-Zucker, Creative Action Network

THE ENTREPRENEURIAL ADVOCATE

When Aaron Perry-Zucker graduated college, he hit the entrepreneurial ground running. It was 2008, the year that Barack Obama ran for his first term and energized American youth with his promise of hope. Perry-Zucker created a website platform for all the artists and designers everywhere to post their pro-Obama posters and graphics. He then convinced TASCHEN to publish it as a book. Since then he has worked with social media to activate social concerns on new and old media. This is just one of those endeavors.

How did you become such a fervent design entrepreneur?

I've always been something of a smart-ass and a maker. I was fortunate enough to be a member of a lot of different types of creative communities that really shaped my path, from the performing arts to communication design. I was also exposed to the work of Tibor Kalman at a pretty early age and discovered the Federal Art Project of the WPA on the Library of Congress website in high school.

I see your Obama poster project as being entrepreneurial. Do you have another description?

I like to think about it and the projects that have followed as explorations in the combination of grassroots organizing tactics and the creative process.

You've engaged in various social initiatives. Do you plan on this as your ultimate career?

Absolutely, but I expect the form to evolve. I've been incredibly fortunate to be able to piece together enough design projects to make it to the age of twenty-six without having had a real job. I like to think of my job as continually figuring out how to be as creatively fulfilled as possible while advancing my education. All of this has led me to cofound the Creative Action Network. The ultimate goal is the creation of some

form of modern-day, self-sustaining, WPA-type network of organized and impactful creatives collectively fueling advocacy initiatives from the local to the international level. We're a for-profit start-up that's focused on developing our scalable model to financially support the creators that participate in our crowd-sourced campaigns.

What is your plan for financial sustainability? Do you have a business plan?

Absolutely. After operating as a design studio for four years and sporadically experimenting with the model that had worked so well with the Obama campaign, we were tired of client work and having to start over on every project. We were hungry to build something of our own. It was specifically our six-month project at Upworthy, launching their graphics creation team leading up to and including the 2012 presidential election coverage, that convinced us that it was possible to scale a for-profit, mission-driven media company, and that a large audience existed for it.

We launched the Creative Action Network at the beginning of 2013 with some money that we had saved with client work and began experimenting full time with different revenue-generating ideas to complement our organizing strategies. In November of 2013 we were accepted into the Matter.vc accelerator program for media start-ups interested in the future of public media. Backed by KQED and the Knight Foundation, this transformative program helped us build out our business model, demonstrate traction, and turn our crazy art project idea into a scalable business.

We're currently raising a seed investment round as we continue to double our revenue every quarter. Primarily, we sell print-on-demand prints and other merchandise through our ecommerce marketplace populated with content made by the artists that are in our network, who contribute to it freely through organized campaigns around individual causes or ideas. We pay the international community of almost three thousand artists 40 percent of all profits after costs. We're also selling wholesale to organizations that host pop-up galleries and exhibits as well as online and offline retail partners.

How is the Creative Action Network run and operated?

Our primary function is running large-scale, crowd-sourced creative campaigns. Working with a partner organization, we invite artists to contribute work to build a collection around a single cause or idea. We then turn their work into merchandise

that we sell to customers and supporters of that cause. With each new campaign, we grow our community of artists, our marketplace of content, our network of cause and distribution partners, and our base of customers. What started with the Obama campaign now spans topics like migrant rights, gun violence, the national parks, and literature in the public domain.

Do you have a growth plan for CAN?

Absolutely. We're barely scratching the surface with our small team of 2.5 right now. Basically, we're working to make campaigns require less effort on our part and that of our partners in order to get off the ground and increase the value of that action in the short and

long term of a campaign's life. We're slowly growing both sides of our machine (content creating, content selling). The goal is to grow and engage our creative community: an organized, expressive, and diverse community of creatives who earn a secondary income by working together to influence the national dialogue and inspire action. Right now, that means being able to run more campaigns that create more value with less effort on our part.

You see the power of graphic design to forge bonds. Do you believe that making posters is a strong enough power?

I think that it's as good a place to start as any. I think that the real power comes from the experience of being a part of a passionate and creative community, from the impact of a lot of people speaking with one voice while still expressing many nuanced interpretations and ideas, and from how far the artistic artifacts that are a result of that process can travel and how many people can see them. It creates a big loop that can be used to bring the content creator closer to the consumer and ensure that a powerful story connects them. And when it's in the form of a poster or something that can hang on a wall or be seen every day, it reinforces that story.

What are some of the high points of your endeavors up to now?

The entire Design for Obama experience, especially being able to publish the collection with Spike Lee and TASCHEN. Seeing how far that idea spread was incredible and unexpected.

Our first official CAN camping was the Gun Show, prompted by several artists in our community in the immediate wake of the shootings at Newtown. We received some incredible images that were seen by millions of people as the debate over gun violence escalated. The most viral was an illustration of Martin Luther King Jr. wearing

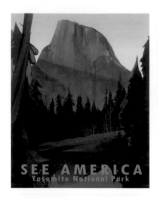  

a hoodie that reflected Travyon Martin's hoodie. After George Zimmerman was acquitted, the image went viral, leading to the artist, Nikkolas Smith, an architect and imagineer with Disney, to be invited on *CNN Live* to talk with MLK's niece about the role of artistic expression in social justice movements.

Our latest campaign, See America, invites artists to reimagine the iconic WPA travel posters celebrating our natural landmarks and treasured sites. Working with the National Parks Conservation Association (NPCA), we have collected over 550 new designs from over 175 artists depicting landmarks in all fifty states (plus DC and five territories). Not only is the new collection diverse and beautiful, depicting many overlooked but amazing places, but it also has generated the conversation that the NPCA was hoping for that can generally be summed up with a tweet like "Looking at these posters makes me want to grab my tent and head to a park."

What are some of the challenges?

We're focused on proving that we can scale our model and face many of the challenges that entrepreneurs face, like needing to maintain growth, focus, and perspective in pretty equal measure. Our more unique challenges involve proving that creative expression can be both a force for social change and that content creators can make money doing so.

What projects do you have lined up for the future?

We're not quite ready to announce our next campaigns, but we're lining up a lot of cool campaigns of various sizes around voter engagement, the environment, money in politics, and a few others. Stay tuned for more!

Kevin Finn

DESIGN NERD

Kevin Finn is a designer and founder of TheSumOf, an independent design practice currently based in Brisbane, Australia. He is the founder of Open Manifesto, an independent design journal unlike most others in the world, which focuses on how design intersects with social, cultural, political, and economic issues. Finn is also founder of DESIGNerd, a card game and phone app. Each of the three volumes of DESIGNerd 100+ (with more to come) includes one hundred personal questions contributed by a specific design nerd/author with bonus questions provided by Finn throughout. The game is designed for fans of design history and other quirky facts. It is "the first design trivia game to feature unique slants on design history, fact, and fiction," Finn adds. "And it's really about celebrating DESIGNerds all over the world."

You began as an entrepreneur with your magazine Open Manifesto. *How did this come about?*

I wish I had started *Open Manifesto* as an entrepreneurial pursuit. Or to be more precise, I wish I had started it as a "conscious" entrepreneur. The fact is, I never thought of it as a business opportunity, due to my lack of business acumen at the time. I was more focused on research, knowledge, and sharing what I had learned with any readers that might find *Open Manifesto* interesting. That said, although I lacked business acumen to make it the success it deserves, I was acutely aware that publishing a journal would be an investment. But from the outset, I was very clear that it would be an investment in learning—an investment in myself. *Open Manifesto* reflects my personal interest in exploring how design intersects with social, political, cultural, and economic issues.

In terms of how *Open Manifesto* started, I had the idea shortly after I graduated from design school, but I began seriously thinking about it in 1995. However, it took another eight years for me to bring the idea into reality. This was primarily because I

didn't believe I was qualified to publish a journal. I kept thinking, "Who am I to do something like this?"

You also have to remember that things were very different in those days. Self-publishing wasn't as popular or as easy as it is today, and it was also hampered by the traditional publishing model. In 2003, I read Emigre #64 "Rant," and that was the final push I needed to start *Open Manifesto*. I thought to myself, "Fuck it! Just start with issue #1 and see where it goes . . ."

Did you foresee a future for the journal? Do you have a business plan?

I do foresee a future for *Open Manifesto*, but that is entirely dependent on readers seeing a future for it as well. I know greater awareness and accessibility are key aspects to *Open Manifesto*'s future and this will most likely lie in the digital space, probably more so than in the printed space.

In terms of a business plan, I have avoided generating one simply because I feel business plans are too rigid, and they are predicated on an assumed end goal that we desire, but which may not be realistic. Essentially it's guessing, and business rarely happens the way we planned it.

However, planning is important. But having a series of plans, which can be used as stepping-stones to get to your end goal, is a better model for navigating all the uncertain terrain you are almost certainly going to encounter. Each plan allows you to adapt as you learn, and this influences the next plan. Another word for it is strategy, but these evolving plans must include financial budgeting, not just action-based planning.

How has OM been funded?

Funding comes through revenue generated from sales, which is put back into the publication. It has also been funded through personal financial investment. I've invested in *Open Manifesto* primarily because I believe in it. And from the very beginning I never entertained the idea of including ads to supplement income. Although this makes *Open Manifesto* a pure and uninterrupted read, it does pose some financial consequences. But I'm willing to live with that and to find other means to be more financially viable.

You've also produced a game series of design trivia cards. How did this come to pass?

Between 2007 and 2010, I lived and worked in remote Kununurra, an isolated town in northern Western Australia with a population of less than six thousand people. The nearest urban hub is a one-hour flight away in either direction. That said, I had a solid list of clients during that period. In 2010, we moved to Brisbane. It was a new city for me and I had no connections there. I was also naive enough to think business would come through the door quickly, simply because it is the third-largest city in Australia and I was able to run a stable business from such a remote location for the previous three years. But I was wrong. The Brisbane market is quite insular, and there are far more studios vying for the same work. By late 2010 I decided that rather than focusing purely on a new business push, I would also consider developing my own product range. Designers spend so much time providing ideas for clients, I felt it was time I applied the same (conscious) thinking to my own business.

Having gone through various ideas, I realized that, rather than just developing a design trivia game, there would be far more value, interest, and insight if I invited leading designers to produce their own personal volumes. I was also aware—due to my design practice in branding and identity—that the product needed its own name so that it could fit within a (potentially) larger suite of products in the future. One hundred questions seemed like a good number, and with bonus questions peppered throughout, I settled on the simple product title 100+. By late 2011, I had moved from idea to development to production and launch, far more quickly than I did with *Open Manifesto*!

Who funded this one?
This has been funded from personal investment as well as from sales.

The packaging is wonderful. How did you decide on this direction?
Thank you. The packaging design went through numerous stages before I settled on the final direction. Since the target audience is design enthusiasts, I knew the typeface had to be Helvetica. Nondesigners wouldn't care (or know) how polarizing this font is, but design enthusiasts would understand and either hate or love the packaging as a result. This was important for me. Although it is a small detail, it is intentional, considered, and a reflection of what the trivia series is about: Proud to be a design enthusiast—a design nerd.

After deciding on the font, I had to design the layout; it needed to be functional but also have personality. Considering each volume is a personal set of questions from each designer(s), I decided to include their handwriting. This helps to highlight the fact that DESIGNerd is a series of signature volumes, and it also helps to distinguish each volume from the other two.

How has 100+ done in the market?
Three days after launching DESIGNerd 100+, Fast Company featured it on their blog. A number of other significant media platforms also featured it. This was

both surprising and encouraging. We quickly recouped the money I invested in the product but, due to a lack of continued marketing (by myself), sales slowed down towards the middle of 2012. I also realized that shipping costs were again becoming a hindrance, particularly being based in Australia, which has hefty shipping costs to the United States and Europe.

I had previously spoken with Stefan Sagmeister about creating DESIGNerd 100+ as an app, and by the end of 2012 began to seriously pursue this avenue. However, I lost my mum to cancer in early 2013, and this affected me deeply—and impacted my work, including *Open Manifesto* and development of the DESIGNerd app. I had also made the decision to stop promoting the DESIGNerd limited edition collectable tins because I didn't feel it was fair to sell a product while knowingly developing something similar that would be far cheaper. I wanted customers to be aware of the choice I was offering: The DESIGNerd 100+ limited edition collectible tin, which is aimed at advanced players, or the DESIGNerd 100+ app, which is immediately accessible, far cheaper, and aimed at the general player.

Can you be a successful design entrepreneur?

Yes. I think it is important to first define success; however, it's also important to define success in the context of entrepreneurship, as opposed to other aspects of one's life. I see success as providing something that enough people feel is valuable to pay for—and which ultimately allows you to pursue your passion in a financially sustainable way.

As to whether one can be a successful design entrepreneur, I think there are plenty of cases and examples that prove this is certainly possible. (This book is a testament to that!) However, like most business ventures, there are two conditions under which success is achieved: First, successful design entrepreneurs are the beneficiaries of luck—being in the right place, at the right time, with the right product in the right market. The second condition is when the designer understands business and is very conscious of the decisions they are making. Unfortunately, this condition is less prevalent, though it is certainly changing, which is very encouraging. True success is usually a combination of both conditions.

What have you learned from your ventures?

Through *Open Manifesto* I have learned so much from the contributors, who include Edward de Bono, Noam Chomsky, Milton Glaser, Alain de Botton, Errol Morris, Larry J. Kolb (an ex–CIA operative), Master Legend (a real-life superhero), Peter Saville, Wally Olins, and Tom Zoellner (an investigative journalist), among many others. I've learned that interviewing someone like Noam Chomsky is a great laxative; I've learned that that I need to separate a hobby from an entrepreneurial pursuit; that I need to learn more about business; that an idea is nothing unless it is made real; that it doesn't have to perfect, but it does need to be thoroughly considered; that pressure is usually self-inflicted. I've learned how to write (at least in my own way) and that asking a question is very different from asking the right question. I've learned how to edit, research, curate, and publish; that being curious is both exciting and exhausting; that being a designer means being a continuous student, learning as much as possible about as much as possible—and sharing that knowledge; that some readers have been inspired by *Open Manifesto* and to allow myself to accept this graciously. I've learned not to spend eight years thinking about an idea and instead to just start; that things don't always work out, no matter how much you need them to or want them to; that some things do work out, in the most surprising and unexpected ways. I've learned to persevere and to pivot; that you don't necessarily need to be qualified to do things and instead to just do things your own way; that simply by doing things, pathways and opportunities start to appear. I've learned about finding my way, falling down, and picking myself up again, even when this is incredibly difficult to do. I've learned to ask for help and how to help others, and that one single email from a grateful reader is enough to motivate me to continue an initiative or project. And I've learned there are amazing people in the world willing to give you their time, thoughts, and support, even when you don't think you deserve it.

What mistakes did you make?

I guess a more positive (and more succinct) way to approach this question would be to list the things I would have (and should have) done better:

- *Prioritize things and stick to them—it's very easy to be distracted by new ideas when you haven't even finished the one you're working on;*
- *Understand business better, and specifically clearly distinguish between a hobby and an entrepreneurial pursuit;*
- *Actively embrace the digital landscape earlier, but in a considered way;*
- *Put timelines and budgets to each initiative and stick to them; and finally,*
- *When you generate momentum, make sure you harness it.*

Patricia Belen + Greg D'Onofrio

DESIGN HISTORY AS COMMODITY

Patricia Belen and Greg D'Onofrio had an office romance, got married, and started their small studio, Kind Company, in 2004 in Brooklyn. Before they became partners in business, they were partners in life. Opening their own independent graphic design studio "was the logical next step for us," D'Onofrio says. In addition to client work, they launched and maintain a website devoted to Alvin Lustig and a design history resource called Display. The latter is an online exhibition space for vintage design ephemera and a bookstore. They've funded both ventures on their own with the aim of providing information and critique to the design community.

How did you arrive at the name Kind Company?

There's no deep meaning behind the name. We liked the sound of it and wanted something a bit out of the ordinary. The two words sound nice together and it's served us well, even in all its different iterations, which some of our clients still get wrong: Kind and Company, The Kind Company, KindCo, KCO, and so on.

What prompted you to start this site?

In 2000, when we first began to discover his work, Alvin Lustig was still a little-known yet hugely important design pioneer who needed to be introduced (or reintroduced) to a growing online audience. We had seen some examples of his works from the books we were collecting, but when we tried to find out more, information wasn't easily available. At that moment, an opportunity was in front of us. We figured the best way to educate ourselves (and others) was to develop a comprehensive website

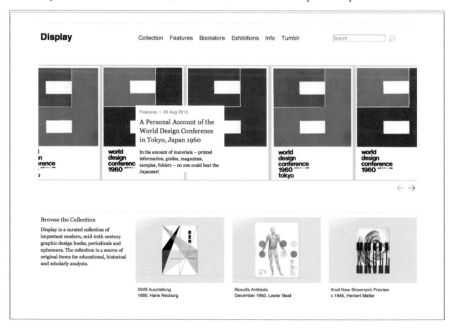

of his work. With Elaine Lustig Cohen's generous support and your published articles, we've been able to make his work widely available to an international audience. We like to think of it as a small but important contribution to the design community.

How do you balance client work with your documentary and now bookdealer pursuits?

Running a small studio offers us the flexibility to be selective when choosing clients. We rarely take on more than we can handle and always leave time to pursue our self-initiated projects, like Display. But in the end, it's all one and the same—our life is our work, our work is our life. After ten years in business, we've learned to collaborate on virtually all aspects of running our studio and make available a variety of skill sets, opinions, and ideas for clients and our own projects.

Why did you start Display?

Since 2000, we have been assiduous collectors of modern graphic design books, periodicals, advertisements, and ephemera. Display started out as a way for us to organize our collection and gain valuable insight into mid-twentieth-century graphic design, typography, and some of its pioneers. Unfortunately, we don't have a formal design history education, so Display was the best way for us to educate ourselves, using our collection. Since its launch in 2009, Display has become a platform for research, writing, and discoveries in graphic design history.

What is the goal of the site as it evolves?

It's become our mission to document, write, and share these important materials. We hope Display educates others about the work of lesser-known designers and the lesser-known work of well-known designer pioneers (the building blocks of graphic design's historical record). As collectors, owning the objects falls short—it's really about what they can teach us. We want the collection to move beyond inspirational eye candy to become a sort of living archive where students and professionals can use the objects for research. So, we'll continue to lend our items to curators and institutions, as well as authors and publishers who require specific images to be published. Ultimately, we look forward to Display becoming a stepping-stone for us to author and self-publish our own materials.

You've made exhibitions. Is this part of your grand plan to educate the masses?

For us, there's nothing better than seeing our collection exhibited and shared with others. The idea of collector as curator (or educator) is intriguing to us. To date, we've had the opportunity to curate two exhibitions featuring works from our collection, as well as give talks and lectures to students and internal design teams. As collectors, we offer a unique insight and a distinct point of view, so curating and educating are things we'll continue to pursue.

You have a very focused Modernist bent on Display. Why is that? What does Modernism say to you?

There are many interpretations of Modernism, but we admire how artists and designers made a conscious effort to reject ornamentation and historical styles, and instead chose to embrace abstract principles, clear communication, geometric forms, and visual experimentation. Most of the contemporary design we admire today (graphic design, industrial design, architecture) has roots in Modernism. The ideology not only lives in the past; it also lives in the present.

Our collection focuses on graphic design as a fundamental component of the dissemination of early to late Modernism throughout the United States, Italy, Switzerland (and beyond), from the late 1930s to the middle of the 1960s. During these years, Modernism's distinctive graphic languages moved away from its political beginnings and emerged as an integral part of mass culture, extending from advertising and printed ephemera to a corporate identity.

One of your highlights is building a collection of corporate identity manuals. Why and what have you learned from them?

Yes, we have a small but growing subcollection of corporate identity manuals, including the Lufthansa Guidelines and Standards, 1963 (HFG, Ulm E5, Otl Aicher); New York City Transit Authority Graphics Standards Manual, 1970 (Unimark International, Massimo Vignelli); and NASA (National Aeronautics and Space Administration) Graphics Standards Manual, 1976 (Richard Danne and Bruce Blackburn at Danne & Blackburn), to name a few. We admire and are inspired by the thinking behind these landmark documents. This coordinated effort of presenting information feels direct and unfussy—and at times, this is a refreshing option.

How is business?

No complaints. Kind Company is very fortunate to have entrepreneurial clients, including small to medium-sized businesses: art galleries, restaurants, architects, authors, bookstores, and archives. When the graphic design business slows down (as it usually does in January and August), our Display bookstore helps fill in the gaps. But more

importantly, it has connected us to students, designers, collectors, curators, researchers, writers, archives, and libraries with similar interests and enthusiasm around the world.

*What does your future have in store
for the store?*

Ultimately, we'd like the bookstore to evolve and grow, and we're thinking of ways to partner with other like-minded individuals or companies. Until then, we'll continue to search for more inventory through purchasing unique items and collections that fit nicely with our interests.

Travis Cain

TOYS WITH AN EDGE

Travis Cain does not make his living as an entrepreneur. But he does make his passion come alive by making alternative vinyl toys that sell in the open market. He has licensed a few with Kidrobot and recently went out on his own. He used Kickstarter to raise the funds to produce the toys. Kickstarter, he notes, is also a great way to get the word out and connect with collectors who might not otherwise find his very curious genre of toy.

What made you start creating toys?

The first toy I remember seeing that got me excited about collectible toys was Doze Green's TRAVELA. It was such a cool expression of his style in a small sculpture. I started collecting a few toys and thought it would be cool to design some myself—but didn't think it would be easy for me to break into that world. I was working for a design firm called Planet Propaganda the year they were chosen to be included in the Cooper Hewitt Museum's Design Triennial. It was the same year Kidrobot was chosen for the Triennial. Kidrobot asked all the design firms involved in the exhibit  to submit ideas for Dunnys, which, if chosen, would be produced as limited edition souvenirs in the museum shop. I designed a bunch of ideas that we submitted, and Kidrobot chose two of my designs to be produced! While I was working on the Dunny designs, I stumbled on expressing the idea of love and pain going hand in hand and how sometimes things (or people) that seem completely incongruous or incompatible often do end up together.

This was the idea behind "the bffs," the miniseriess of toys I proposed to Kidrobot shortly after they chose my Dunny designs for the Triennial. The bffs are objects, like a tree stump and an axe, that shouldn't be friends because one could cause the demise of the other . . . but nonetheless, they are best friends forever. Kidrobot loved the idea and has since produced two different series of the toys and rerun the second series a couple of times.

I have also designed several other Dunnys for their ongoing artist series, including the 2009 Wooden Dunny variations that were the first production Dunnys to be made from real wood. Some of these fetched prices as high as $3,000 apiece on eBay after they were released.

How have they done in the market?

The bffs have done well—the first series sold out in about four months, and subsequent series have sold out as well.

What is the story or narrative behind your new Kickstarter toy project?

I've wanted to produce a larger-scale toy for some time (the Dunnys and bffs are small, three-inch toys). Fun Gus is an eight-inch toy character I have been working on for about four years, and he's finally coming together. The original idea for this toy came from the realization that fungus could be split into "fun" and "gus." The idea for my mushroom friend grew from there. I think of him as a mushroom who has been cross-pollinated with 1980s hip-hop style.

Because producing a large-sized collectible toy can be expensive, I thought Kickstarter would be a great place to try and raise the funds to produce it. Kickstarter can also be a great way to get the word out and connect with collectors who might not otherwise find my toy. My plan is to make three limited-edition artist versions for the launch, plus produce a blank white customizable version so people can make their own Fun Gus. I'm lucky to have had Frank Kozik, Jeremyville, and Buffmonster make versions.

Do you plan more projects?

If everything goes well with Fun Gus, I plan on producing more Fun Gus artist's series and additional characters to make a Fun Gus "family." I am always working on additional ideas ranging from furniture to food, but nothing else is currently in production.

Pietro Corraini

A SIXTEEN-PAGE ADVENTURE

The son of a prominent publishing family in Mantova, Italy, Pietro Corraini knew that publishing was in his blood. And so was graphic design. As a creative director/designer for Edizioni Corraini, he sought to make a mark for himself that was uniquely creative. His ongoing series of art and design periodicals titled *Un Sedicesimo* (translation: sixteen pages) is an extension of his passion for creative accomplishment. Each publication involves selecting a talent and allowing them to do whatever they wish with the pages allotted. It has proven to be successful within the niche he has targeted as his audience.

What prompted you to start the Sedicesimi series?

I wanted to make a magazine that did not just speak about design but that would be a design project itself. There are already many really good magazines that talk about graphic design—I didn't need another one! The simplest yet great idea was to give an empty space to a different author to do whatever he wants in his own issue.

When did it begin?

It began in December 2007 after my graduation from graphic design school, when I was reading a lot of paper graphic design magazines.

Did you have a grand plan? Did you think it would last this long?

No. As usual in my life, I just needed to make this magazine and found a way to make it real. As long as we can find interesting people to feature in *Un Sedicesimo* and find someone interested in buying copies, we are going on.

What is your rationale for which designer or illustrator will do one?

There is not a scientific criterion in choosing a new author. Until now, I chose what I liked the most and which people I thought would be able to make an entire project in just sixteen pages. That's why we mix, in no particular order, great masters like Milton Glaser and Italo Lupi with other young and unknown illustrators such as Esther Lee, Peteris Lidaka, or Protey Temen.

What is it that you want to see in sixteen pages?

I ask the authors to make an entire project in sixteen pages—not just sixteen images or an overview/portfolio of their work, but something new with a strong concept behind it. They are completely free to choose the direction and what to do, and every time it is nice to see what they come up with. Most of the time it is surprising even for me.

i **Mi**ei **A**utori tra disegno,
architettura, cinema, design

ITALO LUPI

Edizioni Corraini

Un Sedicesimo. 2

Is it by invitation only? Or do you have unsolicited "manuscripts"?

Un Sedicesimo is by invitation only! But sometimes I invite authors of unsolicited manuscripts.

How much of your time do you spend on the Sedicesimi?

The really great idea of *Un Sedicesimo* is that I just need to invite the authors, and they do the issue. We work on the final setup and of course the printing: someone is present when the *Sedicesimo* is being printed.

Are you the entire staff?

No, there are also people from the publishing house who follow the publication mainly during the production process.

Is there a business plan? Is Un Sedicesimo *self-sustaining?*

Un Sedicesimo is a project in a more complex context. The family publishing house (Edizioni Corraini) is a company that produces graphic design books and artist books as well as children's books. *Un Sedicesimo* is a self-sustaining project because we didn't need to build new structures for distribution.

After so many issues, it is a "brand." Have you any plans for extending the offerings? Or, say, making it into one book?

Many people have asked us to make a book in order to have the entire collection. But at the moment I'm still convinced that this would represent a sort of ending to the openness of the entire project.

Deborah Adler

SAVING LIVES, ONE PRESCRIPTION AT A TIME

Deborah Adler was first attracted to design authorship in the MFA Design/ Designer as Author + Entrepreneur program at the School of Visual Arts. Over the course of the two-year program, she was tasked with the challenge of developing an idea for her thesis that she could ultimately bring to market. During that time, she says that she also learned how design could do more than delight people: design could solve problems, change behaviors, and perhaps most importantly, change outcomes. She learned to make things and then make them come to life. She has evolved a studio around that social good, particularly in the medical field.

The SafeRx project catapulted you into entrepreneurship, but what form did it take?

At the time Target became interested in my thesis, SafeRx (now ClearRx), I had the unique privilege of working for Milton Glaser. I was juggling two full-time jobs, working at Milton's studio and being lead designer for ClearRx. I was as interested in learning from Milton and doing good work for him as I was in developing my thesis into a nationally available product at Target. Fortunately, Milton was supportive of this initiative and committed to seeing it come to fruition. The whole experience taught me a lot about design, collaboration, and health-care innovation. After working with Milton for five fulfilling years, I decided to start my own business. My invaluable experience and growth as a designer under his influence has been the backbone of my career.

You found a niche for yourself in design for health care. What special knowledge has been necessary?

It is necessary to go to the gemba. Gemba is Japanese and translates as "the real place," the place where the work is done. Health care is now such an encompassing and complex field that the gemba can be the operating room, or the manufacturing

floor of an instrument maker, or the patient's home. There are gembas everywhere. Wherever it is, we have to be there to see all the steps that go into a larger action—like figuring out how much and which medication to take, or inserting a catheter correctly and keeping it sterile (see images). Being in "the real place" where our designs and products are actually used helps us see how to change both behavior and outcomes.

The gemba is where we discover the little things that turn out to be big things. This is crucial for me because my job is using design to help people get little things right more of the time.

The other essential ingredient I need for my work is empathy. Don't create for the world, instead create for the person. We have to understand who touches, and who is touched. Every step along the way, we have to put ourselves in the person's shoes. What would we do, if we were she? What would we feel? What would we need next?

Do you act as consultant, or do you own your "inventions"?

I do both. I head a small studio that brings innovative ideas to market. Sometimes they are my own ideas, so in those times I'm an entrepreneur. We develop a concept, prototype it, protect it, pitch it, and pray. We also work with clients who have their own good ideas, who come to us to make them better. In either case, we always start with the person who's at the heart of our design.

What about failures? Have you had any, and what did you learn from them?

Entrepreneurs always tell me, "Fail often." This is a hard pill for a designer to swallow, but it is a natural part of taking risks. There is no best way to do something; there is always a better way.

Here are a few lessons I have learned. Entrepreneurs can be quite ambitious. We always take on more than we can handle, but most of the time, we figure out a way to power through. Sometimes, however, our time and energy can be limited. Opportunities need to be carefully looked at, and due diligence is necessary before getting too deeply involved.

If your idea is good, don't let it die because a certain party wasn't interested in it. Learn from the experience, make any modifications that may be necessary, and then boldly move on to your next approach.

Moments can get intense and sometimes things get emotional. People tell me, "Don't get emotional. It's just business—toughen up." But I feel emotion is passion, and you should use it to your advantage. Don't be scared to show it. Use it, and put it back into your work. Recently, I was trying to figure out how to get a new idea into the world and found myself in a negotiation where I didn't believe my work was being treated or compensated fairly. I spent too much time feeling sorry for myself, which was not a good use of my frustration. What I needed was to take that passion and use it productively to solve the problem at hand. Keep your eye on the prize and stay focused on the bigger picture.

Will you remain in the health care space?

The health-care world is of great interest to me. It's a space where we have had major technological innovations, but where design hasn't always been considered or challenged. The pill bottle, for instance, hadn't been changed in fifty years. This is a

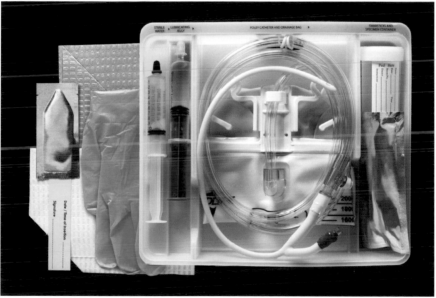

field in which people can literally have their lives at stake, and I feel there is an opportunity to increase care and understanding between care teams, patients, and families. Care is about what people do (or don't do), and to me, that's what design is about. It's thinking about the places where the work is done and making those places our docks. It's thinking about people who do the work and being there with them when they do it. Having said all that, the principles of my design beliefs can be applied to almost any space out there. I have clients in other fields, and I always approach their design challenges in the same way. For instance, one of my clients is a great handbag designer, and going to the gemba for her is a blast!

Ryan Feerer

DESIGN RESTAURANTEUR

Ryan Feerer, a designer and illustrator from Abilene, Texas (feerer.co), is the program director of the Graphic Design/Advertising concentration at Abilene Christian University. In addition, he runs the "properly named" Ryan Feerer Design & Illustration. A graduate of the SVA MFA Design/Designer as Author + Entrepreneur program, he is also an entrepreneur in the restaurant business, a co-owner of Abi-Haus with his friend Jimbo Jackson. Arguably, restaurants are (second to illustration) the most difficult businesses to stay afloat.

Can an illustrator/designer make a good living in Abilene, Texas?

Abilene is a wonderful place to live. There are so many opportunities here, but most of them you have to make yourself. I rarely take on jobs in Abilene unless it is something I'm directly involved with. The main issue I have come across is budget constraints. Most of my work comes from either the East or West coasts, or is international.

Is illustration somehow connected to starting your cafe?

I haven't really thought about it. I would guess you could say that. As creatives, we should have a passion to create. What I find magical about being a designer turned restaurateur is that you have the opportunity to touch all of the customer's senses. You can design their experience with the visuals of murals and menus, the smell and taste of the food, the touch of our handcrafted tables, the sounds of good music and conversation. Nothing feels better than to sit back and watch all of these elements come together, knowing you played a major role in creating it. It is the ultimate design high.

You attended MFA Design/Designer as Author + Entrepreneur graduate program. Did that give you the urge to go into business?

Of course. I learned so much during the time I was studying at SVA. It was a lot of information in such a little time. It took quite a while for me to step back, examine what I had learned, and dive into a big project like this. I would also say there is a bit of naïveté going into this type of venture. Being confident in yourself and knowing you can adapt is important. As creatives we're asked to do this every day. Say yes to (almost) everything. It will be stressful at times, but you will grow tremendously.

You've used some great hand letterers to decorate your restaurant. How did this happen?

I wanted the restaurant to give the community a strong sense of pride with the phrase "Long Live Abilene" as the focus. I'm fortunate enough to be good friends with

Jeff Rogers, who lived in Abilene while attending ACU [Abilene Christian University]. I approached him about the project and he was immediately on board. He asked if we should bring on Dana Tanamachi, also a fellow Texan and friend, to collaborate with us. I gave them my vision and what I was hoping to accomplish. In return they helped me create something much more beautiful than I could have ever imagined.

Are you able to do commercial design and illustration while being the proprietor of an ancillary business?

Yes, quite a bit. I manage my time pretty well, so that's been helpful.

What will be the measure of your success?

As for the restaurant, we celebrated our one-year mark, and we haven't closed down, so that's a huge success in my eyes! Actually, Abi-Haus is doing incredibly well. There isn't anything like it in town. It definitely has a New York vibe, which a lot of people haven't experienced. It is refreshing for our customers to have a nice in-town

getaway. We have had many folks from Austin and Dallas tell us that they wish we would open one in their cities. Our locals see this and have a great sense of pride that something like this exists in their town.

Are there other entrepreneurial activities happening or on the horizon?

For almost two years a friend and I have been brewing BBQ sauce. I would love to take that to the next level, but the time isn't right.

How's the restaurant business?

Everyone wants and needs a good, unique meal on occasion. Our emotions play a big role in that. We want to give our patrons a home away from home. We have several customers that frequent Abi-Haus three or four times a week. They feel loved, needed, and part of the family. We are all about developing lasting relationships and having a good time.

Timothy Goodman

DATING ADVENTURE

Timothy Goodman had no idea that a big idea was brewing when he and Jessica Walsh (Sagmeister & Walsh) decided to chronicle their forty days of dating. Although the relationship did not blossom, the project burst into the popular consciousness. Many thousands—at this point millions—of visits, a *TODAY* show appearance, a book contract, and a film in development later, the project is now the stuff of legend. Goodman is a designer, illustrator, and art director based in New York City. He runs his own studio, working for clients such as the New York Public Library, Airbnb, and the *New York Times.* He worked in-house at Apple Inc., where he helped integrate Apple's visual language, domestically and internationally, and he was a senior designer with the experiential design firm Collins, working for CNN and Microsoft.

What prompted you and Jessica Walsh to start 40 Days of Dating?

James Joyce says, "In the particular is contained the universal." I've always believed that. As longtime friends, Jessie and I always bonded over our opposite relationship issues. In an attempt to explore our habits and fears in relationships, we decided that "dating" each other for forty days could be a way to explore this. Having the boundaries of a project allowed us to take on that challenge. It really was a once-in-a-lifetime opportunity.

Did you see this as an entrepreneurial feat or just a clever idea for public consumption?

As creative people, we love the process of making something provocative that could potentially inspire and touch people. Naturally, as designers and art directors, it was important to us that 40 Days had an identity, but it wasn't until the project

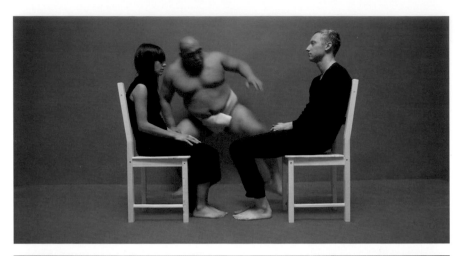

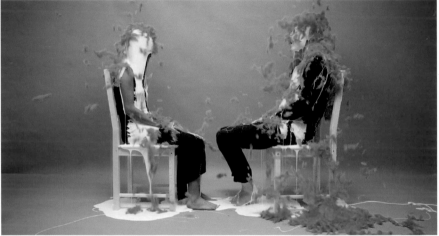

was over that we designed the site, shot the videos, photographed our items, asked for lettering contributions, and so on. We wanted to approach the project with as much sincerity as possible, first.

As designers, how did the two of you prepare yourselves for the final outcome?
Ultimately, this was an experiment, and you can't really define an experiment until it's over. That notion didn't leave a lot of room for preparation for the end.

It appears that you made investments of time, psyche, and MONEY. What was your aim?
If there was any definitive aim, it was an attempt to connect with people and create a larger dialogue. Ultimately, we knew that our stories and issues were not unlike a lot of people's issues. We have since received thousands of messages from people all over the globe, of all ages, genders, and cultures, about how much they relate to us and our story. Many people have written to tell us that the project has inspired them to improve their own lives, to find courage to take charge of their relationships, or to finally date the best friend they've always been interested in.

Warner Brothers has picked up the option to make this into a film. Do you have any idea how this will be done?

We have a great screenwriter, Lorene Scafaria, who's attached to the film. She'll adapt the story, and we'll be consulting her in the coming months.

Do you have any say in the making of the movie?

Because there were so many studios and producers interested—in film, scripted TV, and unscripted TV—we signed with Creative Artists Agency soon after the website went viral. Obviously, it was our property at the time, so we had 100 percent say about who we wanted to sell the rights to. Ultimately, Warner Brothers offered us a great package. From there, we'll be consulting on the film. We'll also have the first stab at doing the movie titles and any art for the film.

Now that it has received so much press, are you figuring out ways to scale up the "product," or is it simply what it is, a fun project gone viral?

Besides the movie, we'll be writing a book that was published with Abrams in September 2014 [*40 Days of Dating: An Experiment*]. The book is a much more comprehensive look at the forty days, as well as who we were before the experiment and everything that has happened afterward. We also want to expand the idea into a web-based community platform, where others can sign on to their own challenges, romantic or otherwise.

It is impossible to anticipate how a project like this will or will not succeed. Is that important in terms of making it?

We didn't really know what to expect. We're not trend forecasters, and we had no budget or publicist. Jessica and I just put everything out there. Both of us knew that if we were going to do it, we would have to do it with as much sincerity as possible, without worrying about the repercussions. I'm very proud that it has taken off, but we never thought it would take off the way it did. It's been sort of surreal.

Understanding Legalities

Little else is more critical to the success of an entrepreneurial venture than understanding the legal consequences. Two experts share their expertise on the law.

In the commercial world there are many shades of ownership. There are also many ways to lose, sacrifice, or relinquish ownership.

Knowing What's Important

Don't leave anything to chance because you do not understand the law. Be savvy about your rights. This section comes at the the end of this book because it doesn't have the same allure as sections One and Two. Yet it is perhaps the most important part of thits book and should be read carefully. Retaining your intellectual property is your entrepreneurial equity; while you do not have to have a law degree, you should be knowledgeable enough to know the right questions to ask. This section is about nourishment. It is also about caution.

DESIGNERS BEWARE

Not everything you conceive or make during the course of your career will belong entirely to you. That is the paradox of creativity in the world of commerce. For designers and design entrepreneurs, the realities of originality and ownership can be skewed. Sometimes your work belongs to others, while at other times it belongs entirely to you. Designers are hired for their skills and talents that will profit or serve a client's needs. Sometimes royalties are paid, but more often than not, other people are in control of the work. Entrepreneurship implies ownership, but to ensure that you retain control of your efforts, you must keep an eye on your legal rights. The following two views are provided by lawyers Frank Martinez and L. Lee Wilson.

ESSAY

Many Shades of Ownership

By Frank Martinez, Esq., founder, Martinez Group PLLC

In the commercial world there are many shades of ownership, from total to partial. There are also many ways to lose, sacrifice, or relinquish ownership—some are by the deliberate acts of clients, others are due to the inadvertent act or inaction of the designer. It is not essential that you own everything that you create, but whenever possible it is wise to retain the controlling interest in your intellectual property.

The first step is to understand your actions. You should know the differences between licensing your rights and selling all rights. What do you gain? What do you lose? When Khoi Vinh, founder and creator of Mixel, an image-making iPad app, decided to sell his venture, he said, "We had been lucky in that the market then was very ripe for large companies acquiring small ones just for their talent. We talked to a lot of companies. Once one was affirmatively interested, it was pretty easy to start similar, brass-tacks conversations with the others. Eventually we settled on one acquirer who satisfied our main goals: return money to investors, procure equity in the acquiring company for my cofounder and me, secure jobs for all of our employees—and avoid relocating to the Bay Area. We all wanted to stay in New York."

The increasingly common practice of buying a company for its talent is commonly known as an "aqui-hire." Vinh's experience was win-win, but other designer-entrepreneurs lack the skill or luck to enjoy similar success. There is an element of risk in any business transaction, so a significant part of being an entrepreneur is to understand how to ensure the security of your rights.

KNOW YOUR RIGHTS AND THEIRS

Once you conceive an idea that becomes a product, you need to make some choices in order to maintain ownership of your creative assets. Depending on the type of work, a copyright or patent may be appropriate. In addition, you should act to understand the impact of licensing versus selling. Learning how to negotiate with clients and vendors will help you navigate this process.

The Copyright Act of 1975 allows you to protect your work, but it must be "fixed in a tangible medium of expression." An idea cannot be protected. No publication or registration or other action in the US Copyright Office is required to secure copyright. Copyright is secured automatically when the work is created. Notwithstanding, registration has a salutary or "upgrade" effect, and is required if you need to go to court to protect your rights. An acceptable copyright notice may be shown this way: © Copyright YEAR (author/owner). All Rights Reserved.

The copyright symbol and notice are not essential under law. Notwithstanding, you should, whenever possible, consider registering your product with the US Copyright Office. You can file your copyright online at www.copyright.gov. Registration is an additional cost, but it is required by a court if you seek to stop someone who infringes your copyright. The registration also provides access to "statutory damages." If you decide to register your work, it is best to register it within three months from the date of the first publication/showing/presentation.

SEARCHING FOR COPYRIGHTS

Searching for previous copyrights may be of some assistance in your research process. However, unlike a patent or trademark application, searching is not critical to success. The first step is to research the available databases such as that provided by the Copyright Office and the online search engines. Follow every lead you can—there is no such thing as over-searching. For the most part, these efforts are almost entirely without cost. Common sense can also serve you well; using controversial, famous, or newly copyrighted materials in ways that are not concordant with the exceptions under the doctrine of fair use will almost always lead to trouble.

Copyrighted works are owned by their authors or by the employers of the authors. Otherwise, the work is owned by those who have purchased the rights as a "work made for hire." Remember, there is no such thing as an "orphan work." It is always risky to use a copyrighted work that is not in the public domain. There may be works whose owners cannot be located or who are otherwise unknown, but that doesn't mean the work has been abandoned or is in the public domain. If an owner wishes to let others freely use their work, they are permitted to dedicate them to welfare of the public by overtly overlooking to exercise any of the restrictions associated with ownership or licensing. Said another way, it is not unreasonable to think of an orphan work as nothing more than a work whose author wishes to let others use it without restriction of any kind. This is a growing trend, and there are now growing bodies of works that follow the shareware, copy-left, GNU, open-source philosophies or otherwise adhere to a "sharing" worldview.

To track down rights, the first resource is the US Copyright Office, which has many of its records online at www.copyright.gov/records.

Stanford University also maintains a record of copyright renewals at http://collections.stanford.edu/copyrightrenewals/bin/page?forward=home.

These databases can be very useful, because a work that was not renewed in a timely manner may be in the public domain and free to use at will.

The University of Pennsylvania offers a similar list just for periodical publications at http://onlinebooks.library.upenn.edu/cce/firstperiod.html.

If you wish to search for patents and trademarks, here is an extremely helpful site. Don't be afraid to use it: www.uspto.gov.

INSURING PROTECTION

What are the useful steps to protect, license, or sell your intellectual property?

First, ensure that all your transactions take the form of documents. If you have any doubt, secure the services of a lawyer and have her review all agreements. Due diligence is the operative term. There are various legal protections available: patent, design patent, trademark, and copyright law. You must learn how your design fits within the forms of protection offered under each body of law. If you need a trademark registration, the trademark office provides for both a written and an online application process, as does the copyright office for those who wish to file a copyright. Remember, however, the copyright office requires that you use their application forms, while the trademark office will accept your own form of application provided it incorporates all of the required information.

If you are using anyone else's material, such as music sampling or incorporating photography or using models, you must get releases or you risk having your project come tumbling down around your ears.

Ignorance is no excuse under the law. If you are uncertain about anything, don't have an otherwise great project come back to bite you. In the fullness of time, the fees you pay now will appear to be very reasonable.

Copyright Basics

By L. Lee Wilson, JD

The US copyright statute states that "copyright protection subsists . . . in original works of authorship fixed in any tangible medium of expression, *now known or later developed*, from which they can be perceived, reproduced, or otherwise communicated, either directly or with the aid of a machine or device." This language allows copyright to expand automatically to extend protection to new forms of expression, including many that the men who passed the first copyright statute could never have imagined. This is fortunate, because the revolution in communications that characterized the last half of the twentieth century shows no signs of abating. Indeed, it may have reached warp speed.

But what, exactly, is a copyright? A copyright is a set of rights that the federal copyright statute grants to the creators of literary, musical, dramatic, choreographic, pictorial, graphic, sculptural, and audiovisual works and sound recordings. Copyright law rewards creators by granting them the exclusive right to exploit and control their creations. With a few narrow exceptions, only the person who created the copyrighted work or someone to whom he or she has sold the copyright in the work or given permission to use the work is legally permitted to reproduce the work, to prepare alternate or "derivative" versions of the work, to distribute and sell copies of the work, and to perform or display the work publicly. Any unauthorized exercise of any of these rights is called "copyright infringement" and is actionable in federal court.

> Under the US copyright statute, a work must satisfy three conditions to qualify for copyright protection.

Since January 1, 1978, in the United States, a copyright is created whenever a creator "fixes" in tangible form a work for which copyright protection is available. Under most circumstance, a copyright will endure until seventy years after the death of the creator of the copyrighted work; after copyright protection expires, a work is said to have fallen into the "public domain" and anyone is free to use it. Registration of a copyright enhances the rights that a creator automatically gains by the act of creation, but it is not necessary for copyright protection. The chief limitation on the rights of copyright owners is that copyright protects only particular expressions of ideas rather than the ideas themselves. This means that several people can create copyrightable works based on the same idea; in fact, there is no infringement, no matter how similar one work is to another, unless one creator copied another's work.

Under the US copyright statute, a work must satisfy three conditions to qualify for copyright protection. All three of these statutory prerequisites must be met in order for the work to come under the copyright umbrella: (1) the work must be "original" in the sense that it cannot have been copied from another work; (2) the work must embody some "expression" of the author, rather than consisting only of an idea or ideas; and (3) the work must be "fixed" in some tangible medium of expression.

ORIGINALITY

The originality condition for protection leads to the apparent anomaly that two works identical to each other may be equally eligible for copyright protection. So long as neither of the two works was copied from the other, each is considered "original." In the sense that it is used in the copyright statute, "originality" means simply that a work was not copied from another work rather than that the work is unique or unusual. For copyright purposes, the similarities between two works are immaterial so long as they do not result from copying.

EXPRESSION

The current copyright statute restates the accepted rule, often enunciated in copyright decisions, that copyright subsists only in the expression embodied in a work and not in the underlying ideas upon which the work is based. The statute says: "In no case does copyright protection for an original work of authorship extend to any idea, procedure, process, system, method of operation, concept, principle, or discovery, regardless of the form in which it is described, explained, illustrated, or embodied in such work." This rule plays an important role in copyright infringement cases, because a judge often must determine whether the defendant has taken protected expression from the plaintiff, or merely "borrowed" an unprotectable idea (or "procedure, process, system," etc.)

FIXATION

The US copyright statute protects works eligible for protection only when they are "fixed in any tangible medium of expression . . . from which they can be perceived, reproduced, or otherwise communicated, either directly or with the aid of a machine or device." The statute deems a work fixed in a tangible medium of expression "when its embodiment in a copy or phonorecord, by or under the authority of the author, is sufficiently permanent or stable to permit it to be perceived, reproduced, or otherwise communicated for a period of more than transitory duration." For graphic designers, the fixation requirement is usually fulfilled automatically by the nature of their work—every stage of any project created by a graphic designer has to be "fixed," even in a rough, preliminary form, in order to communicate it to the client. And every such "fixation" protects the creation, as the law requires and anticipates.

WHAT IS PROTECTED

Most people realize that copyright protects works of art like photographs, paintings, and drawings, poems and short stories, and musical compositions. It may be less obvious that copyright also protects more mundane forms of expression, including such diverse materials as advertising copy, instruction manuals, brochures, logo designs, computer programs, term papers, home movies, cartoon strips, and advertising jingles. Artistic merit has nothing to do with whether a work is protectable by copyright; in fact, the most routine business letter and the most inexpertly executed child's drawing are just as entitled to protection under our copyright statute as best-selling novels, hit songs, and blockbuster movies.

However, copyright does not protect every product of the imagination, no matter how many brain cells were exercised in its creation. In fact, any discussion of copyright protection must be premised on an understanding of what copyright *does not* protect.

IDEA VERSUS EXPRESSION

It is such an important principle of copyright law that it bears repeating: copyright protects only particular expressions of ideas, not the ideas themselves. This means, of course, that if the guy sitting behind you on the bus looks over your shoulder and sees, comprehends, and remembers your sketches for a necklace and bracelet formed of links made from the keys of old typewriters, he is legally free to create his own typewriter-key jewelry. It may be unethical for him to steal your idea, but it's neither illegal nor actionable in court. Although this may seem unjust, if you think about it, it's logical. The US Constitution empowered Congress to pass a copyright statute granting the creators among us property rights in the products of their imaginations so that American society could gain the benefit of their creations. Because ideas are the building blocks for creations of any sort, and because one idea may lead to thousands of expressions of that idea, granting control over an idea to any one person would have the effect of severely limiting creative expression; no one else would be able to use that idea as the basis for a new creation.

Therefore, copyright protects only your particular expression of an idea, not the idea itself. Similarly, copyright protection is denied to procedures, processes, systems, methods of operation, concepts, principles, or discoveries because these products of the imagination are really all particular varieties of ideas.

UNPROTECTABLE ELEMENTS

There are a few categories of products of the imagination that are too close to being mere unembellished ideas for copyright protection to apply. In other words, these categories of "creations" lack sufficient expression to be granted copyright protection. There are several commonly occurring, unprotectable elements of various sorts of works from which the copyright statute or courts have withheld protection. These include:

- *Literary plots, situations, locales, or settings;*
- *Scènes à faire, which are stock literary themes that dictate the incidents used by an author to express them;*
- *Literary characters, to the extent that they are "types" rather than original expressions of an author;*
- *Titles of books, stories, poems, songs, movies, etc., which have been uniformly held by courts not to be protected by copyright;*
- *Short phrases and slogans, to the extent that they lack expressive content;*
- *The rhythm or structure of musical works;*
- *Themes expressed by song lyrics;*
- *Short musical phrases;*
- *Arrangements of musical compositions, unless an arrangement of a musical composition really amounts to an alternate version of the composition;*
- *Social dance steps and simple routines, which are not copyrightable as choreographic works because they are the common property of the culture that enjoys them;*
- *Uses of color, perspective, geometric shapes, and standard arrangements dictated by aesthetic convention in works of the visual arts;*

- *Jewelry designs that merely mimic the structures of nature, such as a jeweled pin that accurately replicates the form of a honeybee;*
- *Names of products, services, or businesses; pseudonyms or professional or stage names;*
- *Mere variations on familiar symbols, emblems, or designs, such as typefaces, numerals or punctuation symbols, and religious emblems or national symbols;*
- *Information, research data, and bare historical facts;*
- *Blank forms, such as account ledger page forms, diaries, address books, blank checks, restaurant checks, order forms, and the like; and*
- *Measuring and computing devices like slide rules or tape measures, calendars, height and weight charts, sporting event schedules, and other assemblages of commonly available information that contain no original material.*

PUBLIC DOMAIN MATERIAL

"Public domain" material is the largest category of literary and artistic work that is not protected by copyright. Most public domain material is material for which copyright protection has expired. Unless you know for sure that the copyright in a work has expired, you must investigate the copyright status of the work before reprinting it or adapting it or otherwise exercising any right reserved to the owners of valid copyrights.

Anything showing a copyright date before 1923 is safe to use without permission, *if* it is a US work. (Works subject to the copyright laws of other countries may have different durations of copyright.) In recent years, the

> **Unless you know for sure that the copyright in a work has expired, you must investigate the copyright status of the work.**

duration of US copyright protection was extended to expire seventy years after the death of an author (as opposed to the life-plus-fifty-years term provided before the passage of the 1998 Sonny Bono Copyright Term Extension Act, which amended the US copyright statute). This change was made in order to bring the United States into conformity with the longer term of copyright adopted by the countries of the European Union.

The best way to begin to determine whether a work is still protected by copyright is to consult the Copyright Office pamphlet called *How to Investigate the Copyright Status of a Work.* You can access this publication and other valuable publications on copyright at http://copyright.gov/circs/. This pamphlet will give you the information you need to either figure out the copyright status of a work yourself or get help in doing so.

COPYRIGHT NOTICE

Copyright notice is an important tool in copyright protection. It is like a "No Trespassing" sign—notice to the world that you claim ownership of the copyright in the work to which it is affixed. The three elements of copyright notice, which should appear together in close proximity:

- *The word "copyright" (that is C-O-P-Y-R-I-G-H-T, not "copywrite"), the abbreviation "Copr.," or the © symbol for any work other than a sound recording, for which you should use the P-in-a-circle symbol.*
- *The year of "first publication" of the work. "Publication" is "the distribution of copies of a work to the public by sale or other transfer of ownership, or by rental,*

lease, or lending." However, the year-date of first publication may be omitted from copyright notice when a pictorial, graphic, or sculptural work, with any accompanying text, is reproduced on greeting cards, postcards, stationery, jewelry, dolls, toys, or other useful articles.

- *The name of the owner of the copyright or an abbreviation or alternate name by which that copyright owner is generally recognized. When in doubt, employ the form of your legal name that you commonly use for other formal purposes. If two or more people or other entities own the copyright, use all their names.*

Under US law and copyright treaties to which the United States is a party, the form of copyright notice that guarantees the fullest protection available throughout the world is: "© 2012 Paul Clifford All rights reserved." You should use this form of notice even if you do not anticipate that your work will be distributed outside the United States. Ink is cheap, and proper copyright notice can offer valuable benefits and protections.

The important thing to remember is that there is no legal substitute for proper copyright notice. It costs nothing, and you don't need permission from anyone to use it. Not using copyright notice on any work that leaves your hands is foolish.

WHEN NOTICE IS REQUIRED

Foolish though it may be to fail to use copyright notice, it must be said that copyright notice is not required for any work published after March 1, 1989. That is the date the United States' entry into the Berne Convention became effective. The Berne Convention is a very old and widespread copyright treaty, but, for a variety of complicated reasons, the United States became a signatory to it only in late 1988. One reason is that Berne Convention signatory countries may not require as a condition to copyright protection any "formalities," such as using copyright notice.

However, confusingly enough, the copyrights in works published before January 1, 1978, the effective date of the current copyright statute, may be lost in the United States if notice is not used.

BENEFITS OF USING NOTICE

You cannot now lose copyright protection for any work published after March 1, 1989, by failing to use copyright notice. However, in order to encourage the use of copyright notice in the United States, the law provides a valuable procedural advantage in infringement lawsuits to copyright owners who do use it. Specifically, an infringer cannot successfully claim that he or she did not know that his or her act constituted copyright infringement if the copyright owner has used proper copyright notice. Being able to prove that a defendant willfully ignored such clear evidence that the plaintiff's work was protected by copyright has the effect of increasing the potential damages award available to a plaintiff, since courts are typically much harder on defendants who have intentionally violated the rights of plaintiffs.

PLACEMENT OF COPYRIGHT NOTICE

Copyright notice does not have to be obtrusive. The US Copyright Office regulations specify only that notice be placed, in a durable form affixed in a permanent manner, in a location on the work where it is reasonably easy to discover. Information concerning copyright notice and placement is available in the free Copyright Office publication "Copyright Notice." You can access this and other valuable Copyright Office publications at http://copyright.gov/circs/.

EXPLOITING COPYRIGHTS

In order to protect your ownership of your work and earn money from your copyrights, you need an understanding of the three ways copyright rights are owned and change hands: work for hire, assignment of copyright, and license of copyright.

WORKS MADE FOR HIRE

In ordinary circumstances, the author of any work eligible for copyright protection owns the copyright in that work from the creation of the work. This is not true when an employee creates a work as a part of his or her job; in that case, the work is a "work made for hire," which means that the employer is considered both the copyright owner and the author of the work from the inception of the work. For example, any full-time employee of a design studio who creates an illustration for a client's advertising campaign has created that illustration as a work made for hire for the studio.

Works created on or after January 1, 1978, by freelancers of any sort cannot be works made for hire unless certain requirements are met. There must be a written document in which both the creator of the work and the person commissioning it agree that it is to be considered a work made for hire and it must fall into one of the nine classes of works enumerated in the copyright statute as kinds of works that may be works made for hire if specially ordered or commissioned from an independent contractor—that is, a freelancer who is not a regular employee of the commissioning party. If you are a freelancer or hire freelancers, you should learn enough about works made for hire to be able to negotiate this tricky area of copyright law.

ASSIGNMENTS OF COPYRIGHT

An "assignment" of copyright is like a sale of the copyright; the author and original copyright owner sells all or some of his or her exclusive rights of copyright for the entire term of copyright or a shorter period. Copyright assignments are also called "transfers" of copyright. Anyone who acquires any right of copyright by assignment can, in turn, sell that right to someone else.

An assignment of copyright makes a commissioning party the owner of the copyright in a work in just about the same way that a work-for-hire agreement does. However, an assignment, or sale, of copyright does not have to be for the full term of copyright. Perfectly valid assignments can be made for one year or three years or twenty-five years—for as long as you wish, up to and including the full term of copyright. This fact gives a freelancer the option of agreeing that the copyright in a work belongs to the commissioning party for the full period of time that the commissioning party believes it will want to use the work or needs to restrict any such use by any other party with whom the freelancer might otherwise contract. At the end of that period, all rights in the creative work automatically revert to the owner.

LICENSES OF COPYRIGHT

A "license" to use a copyrighted work is like a lease of the copyright or of part of it; a copyright owner can grant as many licenses, or permissions, to use the copyright as he or she wants. These licenses may overlap or may divide the rights of copyright among several people. The copyright owner maintains ownership of the copyright because, although he or she has agreed to allow the work to be used by someone else, no transfer of ownership of the copyright is made. Nonexclusive licenses are permissions to use a work in a specified way that may be granted to more than one user. Exclusive licenses grant to only one licensee at a time the right to use a work in a specified way.

NONEXCLUSIVE LICENSES

If a freelancer does not sign any written agreement regarding a work he or she creates, even if it is specially commissioned, the only right conveyed by the freelancer's action in delivering the work to the commissioning party is the right to use that work under a nonexclusive license. That is, the freelancer is under no obligation to refrain from granting a similar license or even selling the copyright in the work to someone else. The law does not require a nonexclusive license to be in writing. However, a verbal nonexclusive license is terminable at will by the copyright owner.

EXCLUSIVE LICENSES

In the case of an exclusive license, the copyright owner grants to another person (called the "licensee") the sole right (i.e., that person is the *only* person who has the right) to exercise some or all of her or his exclusive rights of copyright for a specified time. Again, this right may be granted for a long or a short a period of time, for all or only certain specified purposes, and everywhere or within only a stated geographic area, depending on the terms of the agreement reached between the copyright owner and the licensee. While assignments of copyright usually give the person or company to whom the assignment is made (called the "assignee") the right to use a freelancer's creative work in any way the assignee sees fit during the period of assignment, exclusive licenses usually specify a more limited scope of permitted use. Like assignments, copyright licenses can ordinarily also be sold to someone else unless the written license prohibits such a sale. Anytime a copyright owner assigns or licenses to someone else an exclusive right of copyright, there must be a written agreement to that effect, signed by the copyright owner, for the exclusive assignment or license to be valid.

> Copyright licenses can ordinarily also be sold to someone else unless the written license prohibits such a sale.

See *The Pocket Legal Guide to Copyright* by L. Lee Wilson for further discussion of work-for-hire, assignment, and licenses along with form agreements for each sort of transfer.

COPYRIGHT REGISTRATION

The Copyright Office in Washington, DC (a division of the Library of Congress), is the federal agency that has the responsibility for administering the registration of copyrights and performing other government functions relating to copyrights, such as maintaining records of copyright registrations and creating and disseminating regulations interpreting sections of the copyright statute. All US copyright registrations are granted by the Copyright Office; whether it is a child's poem or a hit song or the screenplay for a blockbuster movie, if it is registered for copyright in the United States, it is registered in the Copyright Office in Washington.

REGISTRATION REQUIREMENTS

The Copyright Office publishes helpful circulars explaining registration procedures for most sorts of works, including *Copyright Registration for Works of the Visual Arts* (access this publication at http://copyright.gov/circs/). After you read the Copyright Office circular that pertains to the registration of your type of work, you are ready to begin the registration process. Any registration of copyright requires a completed registration form, a registration fee, and a deposit of "identifying material" to specify the character and content of the registered work. You should not need a lawyer to help you register a copyright if you read the materials available on the Copyright Office website and the instructions on the registration form.

Although it is not required for protection, copyright registration enhances the protection the law grants automatically. Copyright registration is a prerequisite to filing a copyright infringement suit, and "timely registration" (before the infringement occurs or, for published works, within three months of the date of publication) makes it possible for the plaintiff in such a lawsuit to receive an award of statutory damages up to $150,000 and to recover his or her attorney fees and court costs. Both these possibilities make it much more feasible for a plaintiff to sue. Copyright registration is a very good idea for any work that is of more than passing importance.

COPYRIGHT INFRINGEMENT

If you create any sort of work, you must know how to avoid infringing the work of others. For this, you must understand what rights copyright gives to copyright owners. Only the person who created the copyrighted work (or someone to whom he or she has given permission to use the work) is legally permitted to reproduce, perform, or display it, distribute copies of it, or create variations of it.

DEFINING INFRINGEMENT

Copyright infringement is defined in the statute with a simple statement: "Anyone who violates any of the exclusive rights of [a] copyright owner . . . is an infringer of . . . copyright." Because it is a violation of rights granted under federal law, copyright infringement is actionable in federal court; that is, any copyright infringement lawsuit must be filed in one of the federal district courts distributed throughout the country.

The question of just what actions are sufficient to violate the rights of a copyright owner is left for courts to answer as they evaluate the circumstances in each case of claimed infringement. The body of law made up of court decisions in copyright infringement cases is called copyright "case law." Copyright case law is the source for the test for copyright infringement and the standard for applying the test to the facts in particular copyright infringement cases.

Although any of the exclusive rights of copyright may be infringed, as a practical matter copyright infringement suits usually claim that the defendant copied the plaintiff's work without permission. Sometimes an infringer has intentionally copied the copyright owner's song or book or painting in an effort to steal the successful features of that work and profit from them. However, many copyright infringement lawsuits are brought because the plaintiff wrongly believes that someone who has created a somewhat similar work has infringed the plaintiff's copyright by copying. Understanding copyright infringement means understanding the standard courts generally use in evaluating whether accusations of copyright infringement are true.

THE INFRINGEMENT TEST

Assuming that the copyright in the work that is said to have been infringed is valid, and that the work was created *before* the work accused of infringing it was created, and in the absence of any admission by the defendant author that he or she *did* copy the plaintiff's work, courts ordinarily judge copyright infringement by a three-part circumstantial evidence test.

1. *Did the accused infringer have access to the work that is said to have been infringed, so that copying was possible?*
2. *Is the defendant actually guilty of copying part of the plaintiff's protectable expression from the plaintiff's work?*
3. *Is the accused work substantially similar to the work the plaintiff says was copied?*

If you can remember and understand these three parts of the test for copyright infringement—"access," "copying," and "substantial similarity"—you should always be able to decide correctly for yourself whether a work of yours infringes someone else's work or whether someone else has infringed your copyright.

CREATOR BEWARE

Copyright infringement is an area of real danger for creative people. Consequently, anyone who aspires to earn a living by exploiting the products of his or her imagination needs to know enough about copyright infringement to stay out of danger. People often think that writing plays or songs or advertising copy is a nice, safe job that can't get anyone in trouble. In reality, what you do with your computer or pad and pencil in your own little workspace can land you in federal court, where you will be asked to explain just *what* you did and *why* and *when* you did it.

DEFENSES TO INFRINGEMENT

As in any civil or criminal litigation, the defendant in a copyright infringement suit may offer various arguments to demonstrate that his or her actions did not infringe the plaintiff's work. These arguments that a defendant makes in self-defense are called "defenses." The most commonly used defenses to charges of copyright infringement are that no copying of the plaintiff's work took place and that the similarities cited don't amount to infringement. Anyone who creates copyrights or uses the copyrights of others needs to understand a third common defense to claims of copyright infringement: "fair use."

Fair use is a kind of public policy exception to the usual standard for determining copyright infringement; that is, there is an infringing use of a copyrighted work, but because of a countervailing public interest, that use is permitted and is not called infringement. Any use that is deemed by the law to be "fair" typically creates some social, cultural, or political benefit which outweighs any resulting harm to the copyright owner. Courts consider a long list of factors in determining whether a use is "fair." The copyright statute identifies six purposes that will qualify a use as a possible fair use; they are uses made for the purpose of "criticism, comment, news reporting, teaching (including multiple copies for classroom use), scholarship, or research." Once any use of a copyrighted work has met this threshold test, that is, has been proved to have been made for one of the six purposes permitted in the statute, the use must be examined to determine whether it is indeed fair. Courts often view a fair use defense with some suspicion—after all, it contravenes the instincts of most lawyers and judges to accept that there are situations in which it is legal and even societally useful for one person to use the property of another without the consent of the owner. Don't rely on being able to claim "fair use" of anyone else's work unless you know exactly what you are doing. Consult a lawyer if you are in doubt, or read *Fair Use, Free Use, and Use by Permission* by L. Lee Wilson, which offers a full explanation of this complicated and often controversial topic.

Making and Managing Agreements

By L. Lee Wilson, JD

Design entrepreneurs may encounter several kinds of contracts in their professional lives. They may enter agreements with clients for their services. They may decide to form a partnership with another designer. They may accept money from an investor and need to document the relationship. They may license the copyrights in their work to others or acquire the right to use copyrighted work produced by freelancers. They may enter into agreements with distributors of their work or with manufacturers who produce what they design. They may contract for the services of other artists who contribute to a project.

Anyone who works in business needs to understand what contracts are and how they work. Even if you work for someone else. Especially if you are a freelancer or own your own agency or design studio. You need to understand contracts: how they arise, what constitutes a contract, the effect of the provisions in contracts you are likely to encounter, what you can do if you want out of a contract, and what someone else can do to you if you fail to live up to your part of the bargain. Even though you should hire a lawyer to draft complex agreements and should consult a lawyer before signing the contracts that are offered to you, you will be the person signing on the dotted line and you need to have an understanding of what a contract is and does. But it's not so bad. In fact, if you read and understand this chapter, you'll be at least as well-versed in contracts as most of your peers.

DEFINING CONTRACTS

A contract is a set of legal rights and responsibilities created by the mutual agreement of two or more people or companies; it is the body of rules, so to speak, by which a particular business relationship is to be run. A contract is the agreement itself, not the paper document that commemorates the agreement. In fact, some contracts don't even have to be in writing to be valid, although written contracts are almost always a good idea.

Except in old movies, written contracts do not depend for their legal effect on complicated legal language. The goal of the lawyer who drafts, or writes, a contract is to set out in completely unambiguous language the agreement reached between the parties to it. This generally means that the more clearly a contract is written, the more effective it is as a contract, but eliminating ambiguity may also require more detailed language than most people are accustomed to using and may result in a much longer written agreement than the lawyer's client thinks is really necessary. However, in a skillfully drafted agreement, *every* provision is necessary. Even in the case of an apparently simple agreement, a good contract lawyer will write an agreement that not only provides what happens when the agreement is working but also what happens when it *stops* working.

Sections of a Contract

No particular "architecture" is required to make a written document a contract. What determines whether a document is a binding agreement is the content of the language, not the form in which the language is arranged in the document. However, formal written agreements are customarily divided into certain standard sections.

INTRODUCTION

The introductory section of a formal written agreement gives the exact legal names, and sometimes the addresses, of the parties to the agreement, and indicates their legal status (an individual doing business under a trade name, a partnership, or a corporation). It also gives the shortened forms of the contracting parties' names by which they will be referred to in the agreement ("Reginald Jones, hereinafter referred to as the 'Designer' . . ."). The introductory section may also specify the date the agreement is made or becomes effective, which may be a date either before or after the date the agreement is signed.

PREMISES

The "premises" section of a formal written agreement sets out, sometimes after the word "Whereas," the set of circumstances on which the agreement is founded, or "premised." This section makes certain representations about the facts that have influenced the parties' decision to enter into the agreement. Although it may look like excess language to nonlawyers, in reality the premises section sets out information that could be important if, in a lawsuit based on the agreement, a court had to "construe," or interpret, the written document in order to rule on the intent of the parties when they entered into their agreement and the representations that may have induced it.

BODY

In the body of most contracts, the various points of agreement between the parties are enumerated in a series of headlined or numbered paragraphs. Each such paragraph sets out one facet of the agreement and all probably use the word "shall" to indicate the mandatory nature of the action expected from each party. These provisions are the heart of the contract, since they reflect the terms of the agreement that has been reached between the parties. They also comprise the section of a contract that is most subject to negotiation, since the parties to the contract, or their lawyers, may feel that some haggling over "how long" or "how much" or "who pays" is necessary to reach the optimum agreement. These paragraphs are where, among many other possible provisions, the services to be rendered by one or both parties are described in detail; the copyrights and trademarks or right to use a celebrity's name are licensed for a period or vested in one party; the fee that will be due to one party or the split of revenues is specified, as well as any periodic or recurring payments, such as re-use fees or royalties; the duty of one party to pay certain specified expenses is set out; the role of one party as agent for the other and the limits of that agency are specified; and the term of the agreement is specified, including any "holdover" periods during which responsibilities of the parties continue for a time.

MISCELLANEOUS

Besides all the major points of the agreement, a formal contract will contain what are sometimes entitled "miscellaneous provisions" and what lawyers often call "boilerplate." These provisions look unnecessary to most non-lawyers, since, among other things, they set out methods for handling various events that may never occur, but they can be crucially important. For example, one standard "miscellaneous" provision is the "venue clause." A venue clause states that any lawsuit based on the agreement will be brought in the courts of a specified state or city and that any dispute will be decided according to the laws of that state. This sort of provision can determine whether you sue to enforce your agreement in your home city and state or, at increased expense, in a distant city. Another very common "miscellaneous" provision is called the "merger clause." Merger clauses occur in various forms, but they all provide essentially the same thing: *verbal representations or discussions that preceded the signing of this contract are deemed to have been "merged" into this written agreement and if there was some verbal representation that has not been included in this written document, it was left out on purpose.* Which means that no matter what they said they'd pay you when you were being courted for the project, they only have to pay you whatever amount is specified in the written agreement. In other words, get it in writing. Another provision that can become incredibly important in the right circumstances is the "indemnity clause," a provision that says that one party will bear all the responsibility for its actions relating to the agreement and will "hold" the other party "harmless" for any results of those actions that create legal liability to any third person.

SIGNATURES

The signatures of the parties ordinarily appear at the end of the agreement, after a sentence something like this: "In witness whereof, the parties to this Agreement have executed this document in two (2) counterpart originals as of the fifth day of September, 2017." This language means: *We, the people who have signed below, have signed in order to show our acceptance of the terms and conditions of our agreement that are expressed in this document and our intent to abide by those terms and conditions.* This language is followed by spaces for signatures and addresses, if those addresses were not included in the introductory section of the agreement or elsewhere. In the case of a representative of a business who is signing for that business, this will include a space to specify the title of that person. When an individual signs, there may be a space for his or her Social Security number. The spaces for such information accompanying the signatures on a contract are often considered to be merely formalities of no great import. This is not so. The space for specifying the title of a person who signs on behalf of a partnership or corporation is a good example. If the person who signs is not a general partner of the partnership or an officer or agent of the corporation who has the actual authority to bind the business in an agreement, the signed, written document may be ineffective in creating an actual agreement between the purported parties to it. Seasoned businesspeople learn early to deal only with actual decision makers instead of minions whenever this is possible. Watch who signs *your* contracts, too.

And remember, especially in the case of releases, which are often really short agreements, that under state laws a minor cannot make a binding agreement in most situations. Always insist that the parent of any minor sign for the child. And make sure you know the age of majority for the state in which the release or other contract is entered, since it varies. And don't base any big project on the participation and services of a minor without a lawyer's advice, because you may be left without your talent and without recourse to enforce the minor's agreement.

Informal Agreements

The basic parts of an agreement named above are the sections you'll see in agreements drafted by lawyers. You also need to know about less formal agreements, mostly so that you can recognize them and avoid them. There are three kinds of informal agreements to watch out for: "deal memo" agreements, an exchange of letters, and verbal agreements.

DEAL MEMOS

A short "deal memo" used to set down the terms of an agreement on the spot can be a binding agreement. These are properly used, mostly only by lawyers, to agree preliminarily on the basic terms of complicated agreements and typically are used to get negotiations started, pending the day the basic agreement terms are expanded to full, formal written documents. However, people who don't really know what they're doing also use the term "deal memo" for sketchy documents they jot down or type up during the course of negotiations. Sometimes, improperly, they call the headache they write for themselves a "letter of intent," which sounds harmless and too preliminary to be binding but isn't, because what controls your legal role regarding any written document is not the title of that document but what it says. What they mean to do is write down the agreed terms of a proposed agreement that they have not yet firmly decided to enter. They don't think that they are writing a real contract, but they may be, depending on what they write. If the basic terms of the agreement are included and the document is signed, a court may find that it embodies enough of the essential ingredients of a contract to be binding, whether both parties knew and wanted this and regardless of what it is called.

The thing about this kind of deal memo is that it can be like a gun that nobody thought was loaded. Lawyers know how to include a "sunset clause" in any document that is not a final expression of the agreed arrangement; that is, they will include a provision in a deal memo to the effect that if a formal agreement is not signed by a certain date, the agreement is off and the partial agreement, the deal memo, will have no further effect after that date. This is necessary because of the possibility of becoming legally bound by any written document that sets out the basic terms of an agreement, even if you do not intend it to be the final expression of your complete agreement. But amateur lawyers and sometimes businesspeople who are otherwise savvy instead create documents that don't expire under their own terms and omit many important provisions.

For instance, let's say I am willing to take photographs of your client's new ergonomic computer keyboard at your client's Seattle factory for my regular day rate. This much we agree on. But we haven't agreed on several other points that are important, such as: *Who pays my travel expenses to Seattle—you or me? And do you put the airfare on your corporate card or do I bill you for the ticket? And what do I get paid for travel days? What about the extra days I will have to stay in Seattle if the outdoor shoot is rained out? And how long do you anticipate using the photos, and where? If this is going to be a worldwide campaign to introduce the keyboard or if you want the right to use my photos for more than a year, I'll want to be paid extra, depending on the scope of the use. Or maybe you want to own the copyright in the photos. That's OK with me, but ownership, and unlimited use, will cost you more, and the law says that unless I sign a written document specifically transferring ownership to you, the copyrights are mine. Will I be paid according to my usual schedule: one-half my fee up front and one half on delivery of the photos? And one more thing. I refuse to do this shoot if I have to work for that art director I don't like—can we put you in the agreement as a "key man"?*

Even a simple business agreement can get complicated. Simply agreeing on what and how much and when is not enough. Especially if the agreement is verbal.

VERBAL AGREEMENTS

Writing down and signing agreements that aren't really hatched yet is dangerous, but what you say can be just as dangerous. This is because it is possible to be legally bound by a merely verbal agreement, despite what most people think. If you reply "Sure. OK" when someone asks you to work for a reduced rate putting together a publicity campaign to raise money for a local nonprofit, and you fail to show up for the publicity committee meeting because you've had second thoughts about spending the time necessary to produce a competent campaign for so little money, you could find yourself being sued for "non-performance"—and for money damages—by the nonprofit. And you could lose in court. This is because short-term agreements that do not involve large sums of money can be just as valid as written agreements. Verbal agreements are harder to "prove"—that is, it is harder to determine just who promised what if the agreement is not in writing, but they can be just as valid.

If you think that a verbal agreement you make to work for someone who wants to hire you isn't binding and can't cause you trouble, ask Kim Basinger, who tried to back out of a verbal agreement to appear in a movie she later decided was objectionable. The movie producers sued, and won, and she was forced to declare bankruptcy. It could happen to you, so be careful what you say and never say "yes" before you can see what you are agreeing to in writing.

EXCHANGE OF LETTERS

An exchange of letters (or almost any other written documents, including email messages and faxes) can also constitute a contract between the people who write them if they contain the basic terms of the deal and contain language that can be construed to show that there was agreement between the letter writers. If you send a letter or email message that states "I'd give a million dollars to have you endorse our golf carts," it may be interpreted as an actual offer for employment by the pro you met at the golf tournament. This is so even though you actually meant your statement only as flattering hyperbole to accompany your request for an autographed photo. If the pro writes back and says yes or shows up in your office to say the same, you may have just become party to an endorsement contract.

Be careful what you write in your letters. It's wise to couch your negotiations, whether written or verbal, in clearly contingent language such as "I *would consider* your proposal to illustrate your children's book *if you offered to pay me* half the royalties earned by the book." Never say "I *will illustrate* your children's book *if you pay me* half the royalties earned by the book" unless you really mean it and, even then, you should add a hedging sentence like "Of course, before I commit to any such arrangement, I would have to have my lawyer review your formal, written agreement." More than one innocent has been surprised that somebody thought something had been firmly promised when all that was meant was "I might."

Offer and Acceptance

It is important to understand that the basis of all contract law is the offer-and-acceptance sequence. When someone offers you work or a business arrangement, it is just that, an offer. That offer is just a proposal until you accept the terms of the offer. Then the offer and your acceptance become a contract which, in almost every instance, needs to be reduced to writing. If you turn down someone's offer, you have "rejected" the offer and cannot later compel that person to give you what was offered if they don't want to then enter the agreement they formerly proposed. Similarly, once you have accepted someone's offer, a contract exists, sometimes even if it is not yet documented in writing, and that person cannot simply decide to call the deal off because they think they can do better elsewhere or they offered you too much money or someone more desirable has become available for the project. And making a new offer, or "counter-offer," in response to an offer has the same effect as simply turning down the offer—it nullifies the offer. If the person with whom you are negotiating accepts your counter-offer, an agreement is formed. If that person responds to your counter-offer with another counter-offer, the process continues until one of you accepts the other's last counter-offer, at which time an agreement is reached and, probably, the agreement should be memorialized in writing. This brief account is only a flyby of an area of the law that has filled whole law books, both with the basic offer-and-acceptance sequence and with the numerous rules that have arisen over the years to govern more exotic variations of the basic sequence, such as the now quaint "mailbox rule," which has to do with whether a mailed acceptance of an offer is effective when it is deposited in the mail or when it is received by the person who made the offer. (Usually, when it is mailed.) All you need to remember is that you had better be sure you really mean to offer what you say you do, because your offer can magically become a binding contract without any other action by you.

Words, both spoken and written, have power. And because the law assumes that adults will say what they mean and live up to what they say—or agree to in writing—any businessperson must understand the importance of careful language. In any setting where somebody's services may be hired (either yours or theirs) and somebody (either you or they) will be expected to pay for those services, watch what you say and watch what you write. Or, as Emily Dickinson said, "A word is dead when it is said, some say. I say it just begins to live that day." Emily was right.

The Roles of Lawyers

Sometimes businesspeople think that if they can write an ad or a business letter or the text for an annual report, writing a contract can't be too hard. They will write, and sign, a homemade agreement in the mistaken belief that if both parties to the agreement are honest, they don't need to hire a lawyer to draft the agreement. A contract of this sort is like an airplane you build in your basement—you may not know that you omitted some important step in building it until it crashes and burns.

The main problem is that these agreements are usually not only binding but also probably ambiguous. If you sign one of these, you can end up being bound by the terms of an agreement that no one can figure out without a lawsuit. Owning a typewriter and a dictionary is not qualification enough to practice law, even if you're only writing an agreement for yourself. In fact, who is more important to protect from half-baked, amateurishly drafted contracts than *you*? If you intend to enter an agreement, get a lawyer to negotiate the best terms or draft the agreement for you.

The easiest and most economical way to use the services of a lawyer when you are contemplating a contract is to conduct preliminary discussions with the person who will be the other party to the agreement and settle on the basic terms of the agreement. Then write a file memo for your lawyer, briefing him or her about the proposed agreement and your goals in entering it. Your memo to your lawyer isn't a contract or other legal document and doesn't have to be written with any particular care, past informing your lawyer what you plan to do and what terms you have reached with the other person who will sign the final agreement. Your memo is, rather, an informational document, and so long as it is organized well enough that your lawyer can figure out what you mean, you should include in it as much information as you think might be useful, including some background information. *This* is where smart businesspeople exercise their writing skills—in communicating with their lawyers. Such a memo will enable your lawyer to begin writing the agreement. When the draft agreement satisfies you, submit it to the other party as a formal offer. The other party may then ask for various provisions to be modified or for some to be added to reflect his or her interests. After a little more nego-

You really want to avoid signing an agreement that you haven't read and don't understand.

tiation, you will—or won't—be able to create the final draft of the contract, the one that you and the other party to the agreement will be happy to sign because it embodies the terms that you have previously discussed.

Lawyers handle this sort of negotiation for their clients all the time, but there is no rule that requires your lawyer to negotiate for you. You can review the other party's requests for changes in the agreement, discuss your feelings about them with your lawyer, and get back to the other party yourself. When you and the other party to the agreement have settled on mutually satisfactory terms, you can sign the agreement. This both preserves your relationship with your client and gives you the benefit of legal advice. Although this exercise may seem like a lot of work that could be bypassed, in the case of most agreements of any duration or import, it is not. The more important an agreement is to you or your business, the more important it is to document it accurately.

If you hire a lawyer to draft the agreements you regularly use, you should be able to negotiate and use those basic agreements whenever you enter a new business relationship without incurring any legal fees. Further, the initial cost of the form agreements is amortized over the life of their use and, invisibly, will probably be recouped more than once by the legal fees you *don't* have to pay to extricate yourself from misunderstandings and to collect what is due you. Ask your lawyer to leave an "Additional Provisions" space in your form agreements or pay for a little instruction from your lawyer in drafting addenda to the agreements whenever you encounter a situation that requires special language. But don't vary from your basic agreement unless there is definitely enough money involved to make special handling of the client or supplier desirable. Otherwise, you end up with as many different agreements as you have clients, and your office manager (maybe that's you) will have to remember all the variations from standard procedure.

Many creative people assume that a written contract between people who know and trust each other is unnecessary and that having a lawyer prepare a written agreement in such a case is an avoidable expense. Neither of these assumptions is true. Even if you enter an agreement with another ethical person, a written contract is a necessity, for precision and for documentation. Even honest and knowledgeable businesspeople sometimes fail to communicate to each other all the terms of their agreement. Putting an agreement in writing lets both parties "see" their agreement and provides an opportunity for them to negotiate points of the agreement they have previously omitted from their discussions. Further, a written agreement serves to document the terms of the agreement throughout the life of the business arrangement. Human memory is fallible; even honest people can forget the precise terms of their agreements if they're not written down. And a written agreement can be crucial to proving the existence of the agreement if one of the parties dies or is fired or moves away.

And remember that no lawyer can include any provision in any written agreement that will compel ethical conduct from a dishonest person. The best any lawyer can do is to include provisions in a written agreement that prescribe penalties for failure to abide by the terms of the contract, and even this will not ensure that a dishonest person does not act dishonestly. Your best protection against truly dishonest people is to avoid entering into agreements with them, since a true renegade has little fear of lawsuits, and in any event, going to court to obtain what you were due is expensive, time consuming, and frustrating.

Generally, the more complex the terms of the agreement and the longer its duration, the more it needs to be documented in writing. The very fact that an agreement is in writing can eliminate or lessen the likelihood of disputes. Further, while it may be good business practice to reduce most agreements to writing, some sorts of agreements are not valid or enforceable unless they're in writing. For example, almost universally in English-speaking countries, contracts that may not be performed within a year must be in writing as well as contracts for the sale of goods worth more than $500. And the copyright statute requires transfers and exclusive licenses of copyrights to be in writing. It also provides that nothing an independent contractor creates can be a work-for-hire unless there is a written agreement to that effect signed by both the independent contractor and the person who employed him or her.

All of these are good reasons for consulting a lawyer when you enter into an agreement of any importance. A good lawyer who is familiar with your business not only can help you define and document your agreement, but also can advise you concerning the law that governs your business relationship and suggest contract provisions that can help you reach your goals and avoid disputes.

And need we discuss the importance of care in signing documents other people offer you? Consulting a lawyer can be just as important, or even more important, when the contract was drafted by lawyers for the other party. The old saw about never signing an agreement you haven't read is as true as ever, but what you really want to avoid is ever signing an agreement that you haven't read *and don't understand*. Almost any agreement that requires a written document to memorialize it is important enough to examine carefully before signing. And this probably means having a lawyer review it for you. You should remember that in any business agreement there are actually two sorts of possible written contracts documenting the relationship—their version and your version. This is especially true when the contracting parties are not equal in power, such as when a freelancer is presented with an agreement drafted by lawyers for a large agency. Having your own lawyer in a situation like this can help you feel less like David confronting Goliath. People tend to get very excited about the money terms of an agreement—who gets paid what and when—and not excited enough about other provisions of the same agreement. Terms in one part of an agreement can modify those in another part of the same agreement. This means that the whole story of who gets paid what and when can be controlled by paragraphs remote from the one that promises you a 15 percent royalty. A skillful lawyer who knows your business can often tweak several paragraphs in an offered agreement to allow you advantages that you didn't know you needed and wanted. These advantages can be just as important—or more important, especially in an agreement involving your creative work—as those outlining the payments due you.

Your lawyer can explain complex contract provisions to you and, by negotiating on your behalf, turn the offered agreement into one that allows you more control, gets you paid more quickly, and is generally more favorable than the un-negotiated contract you were originally offered. But your lawyer must be familiar with your business before he or she can do the job you need. If you take your contract to a lawyer who says, "Just how long is a copyright these days, anyway?", it's time to consult another lawyer.

Copyrights and trademarks and the personal services of writers and illustrators and photographers are intangible, but they are valuable. This means that the business arrangements surrounding them must be in writing, on paper, in contracts.

Breaking an Agreement

Sometimes creative people figure that signing agreements is no big deal—that they can simply sue to get out of the contracts they sign if they become unhappy with the people on the other end of them. This is a very dangerous notion. First of all, you can't sue someone just because you feel like it. If you try, your lawyer will tell you to sit down, quit waving your contract, and say slowly and clearly what exactly it is that the other party to the contract has done to breach that contract.

Then your lawyer will give you the third degree. "*Has the other person failed to do something promised in the contract? Has that person done something that is prohibited by the contract? Which provision of your contract leads you to believe that you have grounds to sue? Are you aware that your failure to live up to the promises you made in paragraphs 7 through 9 would allow the other party to your contract to retaliate with a countersuit against you if you file suit? Have you considered the implications of paragraph 12 of the agreement, which requires you to give written notice of any claimed breach and allow the other party to the agreement to try to 'cure' the default that you claim has occurred? Do you understand that paragraph 13 of the agreement requires that you bring your suit in the courts of Peoria, Illinois, where the other contracting party maintains its home office? Do you realize that you could become liable for the attorney fees of the person you want to sue if you bring suit and lose?"* Your lawyer will end this distressing discussion with the question all lawyers ask all clients before they lift their expensive fountain pens to begin work: *"How do you expect to pay my fees?"*

Get the picture? Not a pretty picture, is it? But it is realistic. It may be that the first lawyer you hate if you decide to bring suit is your own, because he or she may have to tell you some home truths about the agreement you signed so cavalierly last year when you still thought you were bulletproof.

Even if you can find a reason to sue and can afford it, and even if you win your suit, you may not get what you want. Judges don't give plaintiffs what they ask for just because they ask. And there are many more likely results of a lawsuit involving a contract than that the contract is declared null and void. One of the most common remedies judges use when someone is unhappy with a contract is "reformation"; this means the judge orders the contract to be altered in some way to cure the inequity the plaintiff complains about. Another result is that the defendant is ordered to pay the plaintiff money damages to compensate the plaintiff for whatever the defendant did wrong. A third remedy is "specific performance," which is the name for what a court orders when it requires the defendant to do what he or she promised to do in the contract. Each of these remedies can give plaintiffs some relief in situations that have become uncomfortable, but none of them gives a plaintiff what he may really want, which is never to have to lay eyes on the defendant again. The law respects the right of adults to enter contracts, presumes that people mean what they agree to in contracts, and hesitates to allow one party to a contract to change her mind and back out of an enforceable agreement. If the law takes seriously your power to enter binding agreements, shouldn't you?

Consider inserting in your own agreements (and asking for in the agreements drafted by lawyers for those with whom you contract) what is called a "mediation clause." These take many forms, but basically they constitute an agreement when the contract is signed that the parties will settle any disputes arising under the agreement by bringing in a third party, a mediator, to decide what a fair resolution of the dispute is. Sometimes these mediators are named, or at least characterized, in the original agreement: "a mediator chosen by two people named by the parties hereto" or "a mediator experienced in settling disputes in the pertinent industry" or "an arbitrator accredited by the American Arbitration Society." Your lawyer can help you specify the sort of person who would be effective in mediating any dispute under an agreement you enter. Your job is to remember that this approach often saves enormous amounts of both time and money when business disputes arise and is a sophisticated and well-regarded way to dodge giant legal fees for never-ending lawsuits.

If you approach any contract with care and patience, you should avoid most of the tangles that contracts can cause. Remember, if a business arrangement involves you being paid for your work or paying someone else or the ownership of a piece of property, intellectual or real, it's worth a written contract.

Understanding Trademarks

By L. Lee Wilson, JD

A trademark represents the commercial reputation of a product or service in the marketplace. Trademark owners often expend enormous amounts of money in establishing and promoting their trademarks. Once established, a trademark may be one of the most valuable assets owned by a company. (Think of The Coca Cola Company; its various COCA COLA® and COKE® trademarks are worth far more than the physical assets of the company.) Consequently, trademark owners act quickly against anyone who encroaches upon their trademarks.

DEFINING TRADEMARK INFRINGEMENT

The test courts apply in determining infringing similarity between marks is "likelihood of confusion"; that is, are consumers likely to confuse the new name with the older, established trademark because of the similarity of the marks? The similarity between marks is gauged by what is called the "sight, sound, and meaning test." This means that you want to avoid choosing for a new mark any word and/or design that looks so much like, and sounds so much like, and has a meaning so like an established trademark that represents a similar product that consumers will mistake the new mark for the established mark. The degree of resemblance between conflicting marks is analyzed by a comparison of the following characteristics of the marks: 1) the overall impressions created by the marks, 2) the pronunciations of the marks, 3) the translations of foreign words that are elements of the marks, 4) the verbal translations of visual elements of the marks, and 5) the suggestions, connotations, or meanings of the marks.

If there are enough similarities between the marks that it is probable that the average buyer will confuse the products or services the marks represent, or believe that the new product or service is somehow related to the owner of the older mark, the new mark infringes the older mark. Confusing similarity does not exist when it is merely possible that consumers will confuse the similar marks, but, rather, when such confusion is probable.

TRADEMARK INFRINGEMENT

Generally, infringement occurs only when similar or identical marks name similar or related products or services. However, this is not always true in the case of "strong" trademarks. Strong marks, because they have achieved broad reputations, enjoy broad protection from upstart imitators who try to capitalize on their fame and distinctiveness by associating themselves with the famous marks. KODAK®, COCA COLA®, and LEVI'S® are examples of strong verbal marks; the Woolmark design logo of the International Wool Secretariat, the Morton Salt girl character trademark, and the Shell Oil Company logo are examples of strong trademarks that consist largely or only of design or visual elements. It is a very good idea to give famous trademarks a wide berth when naming any product or service, even if the new product or service is very different from those named by the famous marks, since most owners of widely advertised and well-known marks protect their trademarks vigorously. (And it is especially dangerous to encroach on any mark that is registered federally, in the US Patent and Trademark Office. Such registration, denoted by the use of the ® registration symbol, gives the owners of the registered mark the power to quash infringers and to recover damages more easily.)

All this sounds a lot harder than it usually is. Since "confusing similarity" is evaluated as if through the eyes and/or ears of an average consumer, you can function as your own first line of defense against choosing a trademark that infringes another trademark. In other words, if you think your new mark might infringe an older mark, you're probably right.

Keep in mind that it is not necessary that a new mark be identical to an established mark in order to infringe it. In fact, the degree of similarity necessary to constitute infringement varies depending on the similarity between the two products or services named by the marks. When the products or services are directly competitive, less similarity will constitute infringement; when they are not directly competitive and/or are sold in different channels of trade, more similarity is necessary to constitute infringement.

TRADEMARK CLEARANCE

Trademark infringement is a real danger for any ad agency, design studio, marketing department, or business that creates a new trademark, which can be any symbol, word, name, or combination of elements that is used to represent a company and its products or services in commerce. Trademark rights accrue by use of the trademark rather than by registration, which enhances the owner's rights in a mark rather than creating them. This means that you must avoid choosing a mark that is too similar to an older, more established mark used for the same or similar products or services. Because both international and domestic trade are burgeoning in the United States, it is much more difficult than it once was to come up with an original, protectable trademark. Doing your best to keep your client and yourself out of trademark infringement lawsuits is called "trademark clearance." It is a process that is critically important to everyone involved in the creation of new trademarks.

When you have narrowed your proposed names to three or four, conduct a Google search. You can abandon any names that are too close to trademarks that are already in use, whether those trademarks are registered or not. An early search of possible trademarks saves the expense of conducting a full trademark search for every possible name and speeds up the selection process by halting your further consideration of marks that are already in use for any product or service similar to the one for which you are selecting a mark.

TRADEMARK LAWYERS

Unless an attorney in your company's legal department or your regular lawyer is well versed in trademark law, find a trademark lawyer to conduct a full trademark search for any proposed mark that appears to be available for use. Tell your lawyer exactly how you propose to spell the mark you want to use, furnish a copy of any logo or design rendering of the mark, and list each product or service that the proposed mark will name as well as the territories where the proposed mark will be used. Your lawyer will hire a trademark search firm to examine federal and state trademark registration records and data on unregistered but currently used marks and will write a trademark search report summarizing the situation. In the case of a mark for a product or service anticipated to be marketed outside the United States, the comparison and report will be more extensive.

Be prepared to find out that your favorite proposed mark is already being used by someone else; it happens every day to some designer or advertising creative person who spent weeks developing what she or he believed to be a unique new mark. The good news is that it is much easier and much less expensive to discard a proposed mark before any money is spent advertising it than to abandon a new trademark six months into your first big promotion of it.

Lawyers' fees buy not only legal services but also the informed judgment that good lawyers develop over the years of their practice. Your lawyer's evaluation of the likelihood that your proposed mark will conflict with an established mark is the heart of the opinion letter that he or she will write after carefully reviewing your search report. In formulating this evaluation, your lawyer will weigh many factors, large and small, gleaned from the information in the search report. Your lawyer should try to accurately assess the chances of conflict, but most lawyers will be conservative in this assessment. If you feel that your lawyer is being overcautious in recommending that you abandon your plans to use a proposed mark, get another trademark lawyer to evaluate your search report, which is, since you paid for it, yours.

Whatever you do, however, don't just ignore your lawyer's reservations and cautions about a mark. This is reportedly what the marketing department at Nike did when it named a new women's running shoe INCUBUS®. The Nike legal department had apparently advised the marketing department that the word "incubus" means "an evil spirit believed to seize or harm sleeping persons" and had recommended that another mark be chosen. Marketing ignored the advice. After the INCUBUS shoe was introduced, somebody noticed that Nike had chosen a bad name for the shoe and stories started appearing in the press. The shoes were recalled at some expense. Nike was embarrassed. It's a safe bet that the folks in Nike's marketing department wish that they had not ignored the advice of the company's trademark lawyers.

DESIGN TRADEMARK CLEARANCE

The best trademarks are visually memorable, even if they are primarily verbal. Think of the familiar, distinctive typeface trademarks for COCA COLA® or KLEENEX®. As famous as these marks are, even more effective are the symbols that immediately communicate, without words, that the products to which they are applied originated with their manufacturers. A good example of this is Apple Inc.'s striped apple with a bite missing logotype. Computer consumers in any part of the world are likely to recognize the Apple logo and to know that it guarantees high-quality products. In an era when many marketers aspire to market their products internationally, symbol trademarks are more important than ever before.

While it is easier to compare verbal marks for confusing similarity, it is equally important that the evaluation of similarities be made for trademarks whose impact is primarily visual. This group of marks includes marks that consist of a name or word that is rendered in a distinctive typeface and marks that include or consist of logo-types. Obviously, when comparing design marks for similarities, the "sound when spoken" part of the three-part infringement test does not apply. However, the absence of this part of the infringement evaluation test makes the other two-thirds of the test proportionately more important. With design marks, whether your company or your client will face a federal lawsuit for trademark infringement just after spending most of the advertising budget for the year to introduce the new logo you designed depends equally on what the logo looks like and what it "means."

The evaluation of a proposed logo starts with a consideration of the broadest possible group of established marks that are similarly configured. For instance, if Texaco were only now considering adopting its familiar five-pointed star in a circle logo, all established star and star-in-circle marks would be examined to determine if the "new" Texaco logo infringed any of them. All marks that included other prominent visual elements besides star designs could be eliminated from the universe of marks examined for confusing similarity because such additional elements would eliminate any real probability that consumers would confuse the Texaco mark with them.

Similarly, all star marks that consisted of realistic drawings of stars could be dropped from the ongoing comparison; all such logos would be dissimilar enough to the highly stylized Texaco star design to eliminate any real chance of consumer confusion. Any remaining star marks would be scrutinized carefully to judge whether the "proposed" Texaco logo would likely be confused with them. If such marks were used to market products or services that were remote from petroleum products or gas station services, any similarities that existed would be of less concern. However, the closer the products or services named by an established mark were to Texaco's, the more serious an impediment to the adoption of the Texaco mark the established mark would be. Even if the proposed Texaco mark were nearly identical to an established mark used to market a sophisticated medical apparatus to hospitals and physicians, the hospital equipment star trademark could be of very little concern to the petroleum company. This would depend largely on whether there was any overlap in the marketplace between the two marks; if not, they could coexist comfortably in American commerce without bumping into each other.

IMAGES AND WORDS

These same evaluations would be made in clearing for adoption and use a mark that consisted of a name or word rendered in a distinctive typeface. The difference, of course, would be an additional important element in the search—the verbal content of the mark. The verbal content of a mark is usually considered to be its dominant element when comparing it to existing marks to determine confusing similarity. However, the visual impact of such a proposed mark is by no means immaterial, especially in a situation where the verbal content of the mark is not so different from that of other marks used for similar products. For example, if a shoe manufacturer adopted for its new line of ladies' shoes the name SWEET FEET and printed the mark, in a script typeface in navy blue ink, on the insoles of its products, it might encounter some opposition, in the form of a cease and desist letter, from the marketer of the SUGAR FOOT line of women's footwear, especially if the SUGAR FOOT mark were applied to SUGAR FOOT products in the same location and with the same color ink in a similar typeface. The verbal elements of these two marks do not sound alike when spoken and do not have identical meanings. However, the products they name are identical. The choice of a script typeface for the new SWEET FEET mark is all that is necessary to push SWEET FEET into "confusing similarity" territory, where the SUGAR FOOT manufacturer will have no choice but to challenge it.

The good news for the SWEET FEET graphic designer is that, although the designer may not have been consulted about the name of the new shoe line, which, of course, contributed to the problem with the SUGAR FOOT people, the designer is not helpless when it comes to protecting the Sweet Shoes Company from a trademark infringement suit. The designer can insist on seeing the report for the trademark search that the Sweet Shoes marketing department had performed before it chose the name SWEET FEET. (And the SWEET FEET designer wants the report, which consists of fifty to one hundred pages of data, including reproductions of design marks, produced by a trademark search firm on similar marks already in use, rather than the opinion letter, based on the search report, written by the trademark lawyer who interpreted the report data but only in terms of the verbal elements of established marks versus those of the proposed mark.) And the designer can, using what can be learned by looking at the existing, established design trademarks in that report, steer clear of any design for the SWEET FEET name that is at all similar to any established mark with any similar meaning.

SWEET FEET, rendered in a block, serif typeface with each letter in a different bright color, may be dissimilar enough to the SUGAR FOOT mark to avoid any potential problem with the SUGAR FOOT folks, who may ignore it and never even think of calling their lawyer. This depends in part on factors that no one connected with the new mark can really predict. One such factor is the plans its owners have for the SUGAR FOOT mark. (Do they plan to expand their use of it, or is it an old mark for an unprofitable line of shoes that they intend to phase out?) Another is the vigilance of the SUGAR FOOT lawyers, who may be in the habit of suing any competitor who adopts any mark that is at all similar to the SUGAR FOOT mark or may, instead, take a more laissez-faire approach to the inevitable elbowing between competitors that occurs in a free-market economy.

The same clearance process is possible for design trademarks that include no verbal elements, but the evaluation of similarities is a little more difficult because confusing similarity may result from more subtle similarities between proposed marks and established marks. The time to perform a trademark search for a design-only mark is after the field of proposed designs has been narrowed to three or fewer logotypes. Then, unless the possible choices are all simply variations on one basic design, commission a trademark search for the first choice design.

HAPPY ENDINGS

A cease and desist letter, which is a nasty document that demands, under threat of being sued, that you "cease" from doing something that is claimed to violate the rights of the person or company sending the letter and thereafter "desist" from ever doing it again, is only the start of the troubles that can befall you or your client if you make a wrong choice in choosing the design for a new trademark or fail to jump through all the hoops in the process of clearing a proposed mark for use. The next step after a cease and desist letter is a lawsuit that requests that the court order the products bearing the new mark pulled from distribution in order to avoid confusing consumers and damaging the reputation of the plaintiff company by creating doubt as to the origin of its products. ("Edna, were those pumps you liked so well SWEET FEET shoes or SUGAR FOOT shoes?") Such suits are often settled out of court, but a settlement would involve the abandonment of the new mark and, probably, the payment of a sizable amount in lieu of damages the court could award. Neither scenario is likely to make your employer or your client happy about having adopted a new mark.

More Than You Want to Know about Cease and Desist Letters

To convince yourself that you don't want anything at all to do with a copyright infringement suit, especially if you are named a defendant, read the sample trademark cease and desist letter reproduced below. It's a scary document, but you can avoid ever receiving one like it by paying a little attention at the right time to the trademark rights of others. For a more complete picture of the ins and outs of trademark law, read and refer to L. Lee Wilson's *Pocket Legal Companion to Trademark* /Allworth Press.

TRADEMARK CEASE AND DESIST LETTER

Romano and Tortellini, Attorneys
205 Waterman Street
Belmont, CA 52245

October 6, 2017
Mr. Robert Wilson
Mountain Properties, Inc.
729 East Mountain View Drive
Williamsville, CO 72984

Via Certified Mail

Dear Mr. Wilson:

This firm represents Brown Management Corporation of Blair, Colorado. Brown Management owns three resort hotels in Colorado: the Brown House Hotel in Denver, the Greenview Hotel in Blair, and the Brownstone Inn in Hopewell, which is, as you know, just over the county line from Williamsville. It is with regard to the Brownstone Inn that I am writing.
Brown Management Corporation has owned and operated the Brownstone Inn since 1994. Over the years, Brown Management has expended a great deal of money to

advertise the Brownstone Inn and to ensure that the services and facilities there are the finest available. Consequently, the Brownstone Inn has an excellent reputation, both within Colorado and nationally, as a luxury hotel. Brown Management is the owner of two service marks, both of which have been registered in the United States Patent and Trademark Office. These service marks are the famous name BROWNSTONE INN, which is the subject of federal registration 1,985,065, and the well-known Brownstone Inn script logo, which is the subject of federal registration 1,985,094. Copies of these two registrations are attached to this letter.

It has come to the attention of our client that your corporation has begun construction on a Williamsville time-share condominium development that you intend to call and, indeed, are already calling in advertisements in national travel magazines and in publicity of other kinds, "the Brown Stone Community." Your use of the name "Brown Stone Community" for your resort condominium development constitutes infringement of our client's registered service marks and unfair competition, since consumers may mistake your condominiums for our client's famous hotel or mistakenly believe that your condominiums and our client's hotel have the same owners or that your development is sponsored by or affiliated with Brown Management Corporation or the Brownstone Inn. Furthermore, your use of the "Brown Stone Community" for your development dilutes the strength of our client's famous marks and damages the business reputation and diminishes the good will of the Brownstone Inn, all of which were developed and acquired by our client at great expense and effort.

You should be aware that the United States trademark statute (15 U.S.C. 1051 et seq.) provides in part that: When a violation of any right of the registrant of a mark registered in the Patent and Trademark Office shall have been established in any civil action arising under this chapter, the plaintiff shall be entitled . . . to recover (1) defendant's profits, (2) any damages sustained by the plaintiff, and (3) the costs of the action.

The law also allows the court to award treble damages and reasonable attorney's fees to the prevailing party. In addition, the court may order that all labels, signs, packaging, and advertisements in the possession of the defendant that bear the registered mark or a colorable imitation thereof be delivered up and destroyed.

Therefore, on behalf of our client, we hereby demand that you immediately cease any uses of the name "Brown Stone Community" or any other imitation or version of our client's registered marks in connection with any present or projected condominium development. Our client will require destruction of any printed advertising or promotion materials bearing the infringing name, including brochures and signage. In addition, your corporation must agree to cease giving out any news stories or causing any advertisements to be published or promulgating any materials connected with the offering of your condominiums that contain any reference to those condominiums as the "Brown Stone Community" development.

Due to the serious nature of your infringing conduct, we require your response to our demands not later than ten days after your receipt of this letter. If you agree to our terms, we will forward an appropriate settlement agreement for execution by an officer of your corporation. If we do not hear from you within ten days or if you refuse to comply with our demands, we are authorized by our client Brownstone Management

Corporation to commence an action in federal court on its behalf seeking an injunction, damages, your profits, our costs and attorney's fees, and all other relief allowed by law, without further notice to you.

Although we are hopeful that we can obtain satisfaction for our client without litigation, this letter is written without prejudice to our client's rights and remedies, all of which are expressly reserved.

Sincerely,
Romano and Tortellini, Attorneys

Hubert Tortellini
HT/tb

attachments: copies of federal trademark registration certificates 1,985,065 and 1,985,094

Appendix

RESOURCES FOR THE DESIGN ENTREPRENEUR

The following is a selected listing of service and information providers.

Entrepreneur Community

ORGANIZATIONS

UP GLOBAL http://www.up.co
ASTROLABS http://www.astrolabs.me
GOOGLE FOR ENTREPRENEURS https://www.googleforentrepreneurs.com
AMERICAN UNDERGROUND http://americanunderground.com
CAPITAL FACTORY http://capitalfactory.com
NASHVILLE ENTREPRENEUR CENTER http://www.ec.co
GRAND CIRCUS http://www.grandcircus.co
1871 http://www.1871.com
ASTIA http://astia.org
THE STARTUP GUIDE http://startupguide.com
500 http://500.co
GOLDEN SEEDS http://www.goldenseeds.com
CISCO ENTREPRENEURS IN RESIDENCE https://eir.cisco.com
US SMALL BUSINESS ADMINISTRATION http://www.sba.gov/content/young-entrepre-neurs-series

EVENTS/WORKSHOPS/LECTURES

STARTUP WEEKEND http://startupweekend.org/events/
GENERAL ASSEMBLY EDUCATION https://generalassemb.ly/education
NEW YORK ANGELS EDUCATION MEETUP http://www.meetup.com/ny-angels
CENTRE FOR SOCIAL INNOVATION EVENTS http://nyc.socialinnovation.org/events-at-csi

Finance

FUNDING PLATFORMS

KICKSTARTER https://www.kickstarter.com
GO FUND ME http://www.gofundme.com
INDIEGOGO https://www.indiegogo.com
CROWDFUNDER https://www.crowdfunder.com
ROCKETHUB http://www.rockethub.com
CROWDRISE https://www.crowdrise.com
UPSTART https://www.upstart.com
DESIGNER FUND http://designerfund.com
CAUSES https://www.causes.com
GUST https://gust.com

VENTURE CAPITAL GROUPS

NEA http://www.nea.com
SMARTSTART UNYTECH VENTURE FORUM http://bit.ly/1OXuVd1

RUBICON VENTURE CAPITAL http://rubicon.vc
BETAWORKS http://betaworks.com

ANGELS

ANGEL LIST https://angel.co
NEW YORK ANGELS http://www.newyorkangels.com
NEW WORLD ANGELS http://www.newworldangels.com/wp/
NEW MEXICO ANGELS http://www.nmangels.com
NEW MEDIA VENTURES http://www.newmediaventures.org
NEW DOMINION ANGELS http://www.newdominionangels.com
MAINE ANGELS http://www.maineangels.org
WISCONSIN INVESTMENT PARTNERS http://www.wisinvpartners.com
TOPSTONE ANGELS http://topstoneangels.com
37 ANGELS http://37angels.com

Education
BOOKS

Blossom, Eve. *Material Change: Design Thinking and the Social Entrepreneurship Movement.* Metropolis Books, 2011.

Cohen, Brian and John Kador. *What Every Angel Investor Wants You to Know.* McGraw-Hill, 2013.

Dyson, James. *Against The Odds: An Autobiography.* Texere, 2001.

Granet, Keith. *The Business of Design.* Chronicle Books, 2012.

Heath, Chip and Dan Heath. *Switch: How to Change Things When Change Is Hard.* Crown Business, 2010.

Heller, Steven and Lita Talarico. *The Design Entrepreneur: Turning Graphic Design Into Goods That Sell* (paperback). Rockport Press, 2011.

Heller, Steven and Lita Talarico. *Design Firms Open for Business.* Allworth Press, 2013.

Heller, Steven and Veronique Vienne. *100 Ideas that Changed Graphic Design.* Laurence King Publishers, 2012.

Hoover, Tim and Jessica Karle Heltzel. *Kern and Burn: Conversations with Design Entrepreneurs.* Kern and Burn LLC, 2013.

Osterwalder, Alexander & Yves Pigneur. *Business Model Generation: A Handbook for Visionaries, Game Changers, and Challengers.* Alexander Osterwalder & Yves Pigneur, 2010.

Piol, Alessandro. *Tech and the City: The Making of New York's Startup Community.* Mirandola Press, 2013.

Ries, Eric. *The Lean Startup.* Crown Business, 2011.

Rose, David S. *Angel Investing: The Gust Guide to Making Money and Having Fun Investing in Startups.* Wiley, 2014.

Vlaskovits, Patrick and Eric Ries. *The Lean Entrepreneur.* John Wiley & Sons, 2013.

PROGRAMS

GENERAL ASSEMBLY EDUCATION https://generalassemb.ly/education
DESIGN ENTREPRENEURS nyc http://www.nycedc.com/program/design-entrepr-neurs-nyc

DESIGNER FUND BRIDGE http://designerfund.com/bridge/?utm_source=dfund-site&utm_medium=link&utm_campaign=sitecallout
YALE SCHOOL OF MANAGEMENT AND AIGA, BUSINESS PERSPECTIVES FOR CREATIVE LEADERS PROGRAM http://www.aiga.org/business-perspectives/
NEW YORK ANGELS EDUCATION MEETUP http://www.meetup.com/ny-angels
US SMALL BUSINESS ADMINISTRATION ONLINE LEARNING CENTER http://www.sba.gov/tools/sba-learning-center

INCUBATORS & ACCELERATORS
NEA STUDIO http://portal.nea.com/studio/
NEWME http://www.newmeaccelerator.com
MANOS ACCELERATOR http://www.manosaccelerator.com
STARTUP NEXT http://www.startupnext.co
GOOGLE FOR ENTREPRENEURS https://www.googleforentrepreneurs.com
ANGELPAD http://angelpad.org
TECHSTARS http://www.techstars.com/program/locations/nyc/
BEESPACE http://www.beespacenyc.org
BLUE RIDGE FOUNDATION http://brfny.org
CENTRE FOR SOCIAL INNOVATION http://nyc.socialinnovation.org
DREAMIT VENTURES http://www.dreamitventures.com
ENTREPRENEURS ROUNDTABLE ACCELERATOR http://eranyc.com
FINTECH INNOVATION LAB http://www.fintechinnovationlab.com
INTERPLAY http://www.interplay.vc
NIKE FUEL LAB http://www.nikefuellab.com
SAMSUNG ACCELERATOR http://samsungaccelerator.com
START CO. http://neverstop.co
THE DAILY NEWS INNOVATION LAB http://www.lab.nydailynews.com
FOUNDERS PAD http://www.founderspad.com
FASHION TECHNOLOGY ACCELERATOR http://www.ftaccelerator.com
NYC SEED START http://nycseedstart.com

Index